I0559389

What Language Shall I Borrow?

Sermons by

James S. Currie

Parson's Porch Books

What Language Shall I Borrow?

ISBN: Softcover 978-1-960326-80-5

Copyright © 2024 by James S. Currie

All rights reserved. No part of this book may be reproduced or transmitted in any form or by any means, electronic or mechanical, including photocopying, recording, or by any information storage and retrieval system, without permission in writing from the publisher.

Parson's Porch Books is an imprint of Parson's Porch & Company (PP&C) in Cleveland, Tennessee. PP&C is a self-funded charity which earns money by publishing books of noted authors, representing all genres. Its face and voice is **David Russell Tullock** who you can contact at: dtullock@parsonsporch.com.

Parson's Porch & Company *turns books into bread & milk* by sharing its profits with the poor.

www.parsonsporch.com

What Language Shall I Borrow?

Dedicated to the memory of

Margaret Carlyle Currie Plunkett

and

Steve Whitson Plunkett

Contents

Preface

These sermons were preached in the second decade of the 21st century at First Presbyterian Church, Pasadena, Texas. The eight years I was privileged to serve as the pastor of that congregation were ones in which, together, we joyfully sought to be the people of God in our thoughts, questions, struggles, and actions. That congregation is a winsome reflection of the answer to the first question in the Westminster Shorter Catechism, namely, our "chief end is to glorify God and enjoy Him forever." That may look different in different congregations, but the grace and goodness shown in Pasadena were – and are – certainly important reflections of the gospel.

I understand that sermons are to be preached and heard by a particular congregation at a particular time and a particular place. However, it might also be the case that something of the gospel might shine through in the reading of them in another context. I have certainly learned from and been inspired by reading sermons by others long after they were actually preached.

Finally, lest the sin of egotism enter the picture too much, it must be said that these sermons were aimed at me as much as at anyone. Nevertheless, it is hoped that they convey something of the gospel that is helpful and, in these challenging days, offer a word of encouragement, hope and grace.

James S. ("Jim") Currie
Easter 2024

St. Kilda

Ezekiel 37:1-14

April 6, 2014

The hand of the Lord came upon me, and brought me out by the spirit of the Lord and set me down in the middle of a valley; it was full of bones. He led me all around them; there were very many lying in the valley, and they were very dry. He said to me, "Mortal, can these bones live?" I answered, "O Lord God, you know." Then he said to me, "Prophesy to these bones, and say to them: O dry bones, hear the word of the Lord. Thus says the Lord God to these bones: I will cause breath to enter you, and you shall live. I will lay sinews on you, and will cause flesh to come upon you, and cover you with skin, and put breath in you, and you shall live; and you shall know that I am the Lord."

So I prophesied as I had been commanded; and as I prophesied, suddenly there was a noise, a rattling, and the bones came together, bone to its bone. I looked, and there were sinews on them, and flesh had come upon them, and skin had covered them; but there was no breath in them. Then he said to me, "Prophesy to the breath, prophesy, mortal, and say to the breath: Thus says the Lord God: Come from the four winds, O breath, and breathe upon these slain, that they may live." I prophesied as he commanded me, and the breath came into them, and they lived, and stood on their feet, a vast multitude.

Then he said to me, "Mortal, these bones are the whole house of Israel. They say, 'Our bones are dried up, and our hope is lost; we are cut off completely.' Therefore prophesy and say to them, Thus says the Lord God: I am going to open your graves, O my people; and I will bring you back to the land of Israel. And you shall know that I am the Lord, when I open your graves, and bring you up from your graves, O my people. I will put my spirit within you, and you shall live, and I will place you on your own soil; then you shall know that I, the Lord, have spoken and will act," says the Lord.

Have you ever bought a book on a subject about which you knew absolutely nothing, but on a lark you decided to buy it because the subject looked interesting? It's happened to me more than once, but it happened on our recent trip to Scotland. Our tour bus pulled into Oban, the day before we were to go to the island of Iona. We arrived in Oban a little before 5 p.m. After checking into the hotel, I ran down the street to a bookstore that we had passed coming into town and would close at 5:30 p.m. Among other things, I saw several books on a place called St. Kilda. Initially, I thought St. Kilda was a person about whom I knew nothing, but then I discovered that St. Kilda was an isolated group of islands, located in the North Atlantic, about 40 miles beyond the Outer Hebrides. It is the most remote part of the British Isles. From what I can tell there was never any saint named Kilda, so the origin of the name remains something of a mystery.

The book that I bought in that bookstore in Oban was titled *The Life & Death of St. Kilda: The Moving Story of a Vanished Island Community* by Tom Steel. It seems that there has been a community of people living on the main island of Hirta for as long as 2,000 years. The population never exceeded 180 people. People survived mostly on sea birds and sheep. There are no trees on any of the islands. The people would have to store food for as much as six months, especially during the winter months. Everyone lived and worked together. The division of labor among men, women, and children was clear. At least until the middle of the 19th century there was little or no communication with the world beyond those tiny islands. And even in the 19th century communication was often only by lighting a fire at the top of a mountain in hopes that a passing ship might see it.

For a variety of reasons, some good and some questionable, in 1930 the residents of St. Kilda were evacuated from those islands and relocated to the mainland of Scotland and England.

Over the years missionaries were sent to St. Kilda. After the Church of Scotland divided in 1843 and the Free Church broke away, most of the missionaries came from the Free Church of Scotland, a much more conservative branch of the Church. There was a point in the book at which my heart broke as I read about the influence of the 19th century missionaries on the St. Kildans. The residents of St. Kilda admired and respected all the missionaries that came to the islands. All the missionaries were much better educated than the St. Kildans. However, as much good as many of the Free Church missionaries did, Steel writes that not all the changes were positive. With the arrival of one missionary, John MacDonald, Steel says, "The St. Kildans lost their sense of gaiety and their love of song and dance" (p. 95). Steel goes on to quote one observer, the St. Kildans "do not appear like good people going to listen to glad tidings of great joy, but like a troop of the damned whom Satan is driving to the bottomless pit" (p. 99).

As I read that, several thoughts occurred to me. One was, how sad it is that the good news of the gospel is often presented as bad news. While it's true that we need to be reminded of our own sinful nature and our need for God's saving grace, it's also true that that grace enables us to move beyond a permanent state of guilt to one of joy and gratitude and happy service.

Another thought was how sad it was that the sense of gaiety and a love for music, song, and dance was killed by something that was supposed to be happy, comforting, and joyful.

And then, as I reflected on the story of the valley of dry bones we read this morning in Ezekiel, I thought about St. Kilda. However, instead of watching the dry bones come to life, as is the case in Ezekiel, we see the reverse in St. Kilda where the lively, joyful bones dry up.

It's important to remember that it's the Spirit, not the church, that gives life. It's the Spirit that breathes life into each of us. It's the Spirit that brought the church into being on that first Pentecost. It's the Spirit that enables us to experience the grace and love of God. It's the Spirit of the law, not the letter, that Jesus emphasizes. He is more interested in sharing and reflecting God's love than in saying or believing the right thing.

Now, as a Presbyterian, I happen to believe that what we believe matters. It matters a lot. But none of that matters if in our day-to-day lives we don't live the gospel, if the gospel doesn't come alive in who we are and how we live. Helen Keller was once asked if there was anything worse than losing your sight. She said, "Yes, losing your vision." If we say the right things, but don't either believe them or live them as a vision for ourselves, then we are lost, perhaps even dead.

That's what happened to Ezekiel's listeners, is it not? Even though Nebuchadnezzar, king of Babylon, had captured Jerusalem and had taken many of Israel's leaders, including Ezekiel himself, as hostages to Babylon, all must have seemed lost to those around Ezekiel. Not only no homeland, not only no temple, but now held hostage in a foreign country. Even if they had looked back to the glory days of David 500 years earlier, that must have seemed more like a dream than like a reality. The past was dead and now the present seemed just as dead. "By the waters of Babylon -- there we sat down and wept when we remembered Zion", the psalmist writes (Psalm 137:1).

And what was Ezekiel's message? God can do the impossible, even resurrect the dead. "Can these bones live?" And just as God had breathed life into the first human beings, God now breathes new life into dry, parched, dead bones. Ezekiel kept the vision before those Israelite exiles, that they had been claimed by the God of life and new life, the God who promised to be faithful in good times and in desperate times, the God who never deserts God's creation, the God who claimed them as God's own.

The folks of St. Kilda loved their land. There was a certain joy in their life and work, as isolated and remote as they might have been. There was an acceptance of who they were and of their environment and the way they cared for and supported each other that reflected a love for God and God's creation as well as for each other.

That's one of the things I admire and love about this congregation. You are open to new experiences and to new ideas. We may reject them, but you are open to them. You are open to trying new things. That brings growth. Whether it's hearing about the issue of human trafficking and being willing to host an art exhibit that promotes awareness of that issue or hosting a totally different kind of worship than that to which we are accustomed, like the gospel music we experienced last weekend. You exhibited an open mind. I think most of those who experienced last weekend found it refreshing and invigorating. Not everyone did. One or two came up to me after worship on Sunday and observed, "Well, that was different."

Someone once said that the purpose of education is to replace an empty mind with an open mind. Whatever it is may or may not be our cup of tea, but you have been open to it and have experienced it and can now reflect on and talk about it with some degree of appreciation for the larger church and the world. At the very least, we have experienced how other believers in the Christian faith worship the same God we worship. Our world has expanded, and that is a good thing. That's the Spirit at work. That's keeping the vision of God's presence in the world before us. That's breathing new life into dry bones.

At the presbytery meeting a couple of weeks ago someone was asking about what was going on here at First Presbyterian Church in Pasadena. It was such fun telling them about everything that was going on now and had been going on for the past six months or so. Someone from this church at the table said," The church is so alive!" I had to agree and was so pleased, probably sinfully so, to be part of such an active and lively congregation.

Someone once said something to the effect, "It doesn't matter where you're walking to preach if your preaching isn't in your walking." I'd much rather be part of a congregation that is alive, vibrant, and open to trying new things than to think we're playing it safe by doing little or nothing. The first one is a reflection of God's Spirit at work, while the second refuses to trust the Spirit.

"Mortal, can these bones live?" When the word of the Lord is spoken, heard, trusted, and received, dead bones can not only live again, but they can thrive. As we move through this Lenten season, may we grow in our trust of the Spirit, so that as we approach the cross and the empty tomb, we may move from heartfelt repentance to Spirit-filled joy and gratitude, living each day fully present to the present and seeing what is before us as an opportunity to serve God and one another.

Thanks be to God!

Showing Up

John 20:19-31

April 27, 2014

When it was evening on that day, the first day of the week, and the doors of the house where the disciples had met were locked for fear of the Jews, Jesus came and stood among them and said, "Peace be with you." After he said this, he showed them his hands and his side. Then the disciples rejoiced when they saw the Lord. Jesus said to them again, "Peace be with you. As the Father has sent me, so I send you." When he had said this, he breathed on them and said to them, "Receive the Holy Spirit. If you forgive the sins of any, they are forgiven them; if you retain the sins of any, they are retained."

But Thomas (who was called the Twin), one of the twelve, was not with them when Jesus came. So the other disciples told him, "We have seen the Lord." But he said to them, "Unless I see the mark of the nails in his hands, and put my finger in the mark of the nails and my hand in his side, I will not believe."

A week later his disciples were again in the house, and Thomas was with them. Although the doors were shut, Jesus came and stood among them and said, "Peace be with you." Then he said to Thomas, "Put your finger here and see my hands. Reach out your hand and put it in my side. Do not doubt but believe." Thomas answered him, "My Lord and my God!" Jesus said to him, "Have you believed because you have seen me? Blessed are those who have not seen and yet have come to believe."

Now Jesus did many other signs in the presence of his disciples, which are not written in this book. But these are written so that you may come to believe that Jesus is the Messiah, the Son of God, and that through believing you may have life in his name.

Last Sunday morning I was at Crenshaw Park around 6:15 for the 7 a.m. Easter Sunrise service. I had arrived that early because I had been told that some of the musicians wanted to get in and set up around 6:30. Since I had the paperwork for the reservation, I needed to be there early enough to give the paperwork to the gentleman from the city who would unlock the gate to the pavilion. We waited for the gentleman from the city to arrive. 6:30 came and went. 6:40 came and went. 6:45 came and went. Some of us were getting a bit nervous. Paranoid that some of us can be, we thought that maybe we had been forgotten, and we were imagining a sunrise service in the parking lot -- which was always possible, but not exactly what we had planned. All the chairs had been set up and were waiting for us, but we could not get in. 6:50 came and still no one to unlock the gate. Finally, around 6:55 the gentleman showed up -- right on time as far as he was concerned -- and let us in. He was gracious and courteous, but several of us had wondered if anyone was going to come and let us in. After all, the churches had paid their money, and someone had always been there in years past. All that worry for naught. The man showed up just as the agreement stipulated, and everything came off just as it was supposed to.

Woody Allen famously said that eighty percent of success in life is showing up. This past week I thanked someone for coming to a certain event. Her response? "That's what it's all about, isn't it -- showing up." Someone else has said, "Most of life is showing up. You do the best you can, which varies from day to day" (Regina Brett).

All of us have had the experience, at one time or another, of someone not showing up – perhaps we were the ones who didn't show up. It can be embarrassing, it can be frustrating, and it can cause someone to lose confidence in a person's reliability. And sometimes there can be a perfectly good explanation which changes our perspective altogether.

In the passage we read this morning more often than not the focus of attention is on Thomas and his unwillingness to believe that Jesus had truly risen from the dead. In all candor I probably would have been right there with Thomas. I suspect that most people today would find it equally unbelievable. Unless we can see it with our own eyes, we won't believe it. After all, seeing is believing, isn't it? Not in the Christian faith. The reverse is actually the case: believing is seeing. Until we believe it, we'll never see it.

But enough sermons have been preached and enough ink has been spilled on Thomas. There is another aspect to this text that strikes me as particularly important that is often overlooked or, better said, taken for granted. And that is simply the fact that Jesus "came and stood among them", as John puts it. The disciples had locked themselves in a house for fear that they still might be endangered by virtue of their relationship with Jesus.

So, Jesus shows up. Is this good news or not? If the disciples were afraid of being endangered because they had been associated with Jesus, could it be that now they were in even more danger since Jesus was actually there? Perhaps, but they did not seem to care. Here was the one who had loved them and whom they had loved and followed. Here was the one who had been crucified, who had been dead and buried. Here, in fact, was the one who had risen from the grave just as he had said he would.

He returns a week later. In the meantime Thomas is told that he missed out on seeing Jesus. Yeah, right. Then Jesus shows up again when the disciples are in the same house. Knowing of Thomas' skepticism, Jesus invites him to touch the scars in his hands where the nails had been driven and in his side where the soldiers had pierced him with their swords. "My Lord and my God!" Thomas declares. To which Jesus replies, "Blessed are those who have not seen and yet have come to believe."

Jesus showed up. When those disciples were confused, depressed, afraid, Jesus showed up. One person has written the following: "I'm unfinished. I'm unfixed. And the reality is that's where God meets me in the mess of my life, in the unfixedness, in the brokenness. I thought he did the opposite, he got rid of all that stuff. But if you read the Bible, if you look at it at all, constantly he was showing up in people's lives at the worst possible time of their life" (quote from Mark Yaconelli).

That's true. That's the gospel. The sad thing is that we, like Thomas, refuse to believe in order to see. We refuse to open our eyes to the presence of God in our midst. The risen Christ is here. Now. The risen Christ is in the world. The risen Christ is in the doctor's office and in the hospital room. The risen Christ shows up in our offices and in board rooms. The risen Christ is in the grocery store and in the post office. He's not there to "fix" things. He's there to bring strength, to bring patience and grace, to bring completeness and wholeness to our brokenness. Just when we are at our wits end, just when we think we cannot believe anything anymore, just when we are convinced that the doubters are right, the risen Christ shows up. Or, perhaps better said, our eyes are opened to see him who is already there.

And what is our response? "My Lord and my God!" But we are called to go beyond that. We are called to show up for others. What does that look like? It can look like all kinds of things. It can look like a hug or a word of comfort to a young person whose father has recently and suddenly died. It can look like a meal to someone whose child has suffered a horrible accident. It can look like a word of encouragement to someone about to give up on a project long in the making. It can look like keeping one's word to do something even if you think no one would notice if you didn't do it.

Or it can look like this. I have two very good friends, both of whom attended a small Presbyterian college many years ago. The two of them were like brothers. The one was going through a particularly bad time. He was confused. He was angry. He didn't really care much about going to class. He was drinking a lot. One day he told his friend he had to leave. He was going to see his girlfriend in Missouri. He was disheveled, he smelled, he was depressed. He was gone for a couple of weeks. Finally, in the middle of night he called his friend who was still at the college. He said, "Come get me. I'm at the bus station in Memphis." So, his friend immediately got up and drove for the couple of hours to the Memphis Greyhound bus station and picked up his friend. The drive back to the college was a quiet one with neither one saying much to the other. Finally, the one who had left town simply turned to his friend and said, "Thanks for showing up." As the sun was coming up in the east, the two stopped at a local cafe and got a bite to eat. Both of those friends went on to finish college, seminary, and entered the ministry.

Thanks for showing up. Jesus shows up. Can we, with the eyes of faith, see him and listen to him? And will we show up for others? That's what we are called to do. Are we there for our children? Are we there for our parents? Are we there for our siblings? Are we there for our neighbor? Are we there for the church?

"Have you believed because you have seen me?" Jesus asks. "Blessed are those who have not seen and yet have come to believe." Believing, may we see the risen Christ in our midst and respond with joyful service. As he has shown up, may we also.

Thanks be to God!

Lux Lucet in Tenebris

John 1:1-14

September 28, 2014

In the beginning was the Word, and the Word was with God, and the Word was God. He was in the beginning with God. All things came into being through him, and without him not one thing came into being. What has come into being in him was life, and the life was the light of all people. The light shines in the darkness, and the darkness did not overcome it.

There was a man sent from God, whose name was John. He came as a witness to testify to the light, so that all might believe through him. He himself was not the light, but he came to testify to the light. The true light, which enlightens everyone, was coming into the world.

He was in the world, and the world came into being through him; yet the world did not know him. He came to what was his own, and his own people did not accept him. But to all who received him, who believed in his name, he gave power to become children of God, who were born, not of blood or of the will of the flesh or of the will of man, but of God.

And the Word became flesh and lived among us, and we have seen his glory, the glory as of a father's only son, full of grace and truth.

It was the summer of 1967. I had finished my first summer job. I was working as a lifeguard at the pool at Mo-Ranch and being a general all-round flunky. A friend of mine who had been at Mo-Ranch that summer was a student at Austin College and was in Houston at the time. While he was in Houston we went to see the movie that had just come out, "In the Heat of the Night" which starred Rod Steiger and Sidney Poitier. Steiger plays the sheriff in the town of Sparta, Mississippi where a murder has occurred. Poitier plays a black homicide investigator, Virgil Tibbs, from Philadelphia, Pennsylvania and just happens to be passing through Sparta on his way back to Philadelphia from visiting his mother after this murder has occurred.

The summer of 1967 is known to some as "the long hot summer" because 159 race riots occurred across this country -- from Boston to Detroit to Tampa to Birmingham to Newark to Milwaukee to New York, among other cities. As a result of this racial unrest, President Johnson established the Kerner Commission to investigate the underlying causes of the riots.

So, my friend and I went to see this movie at the Majestic Theater near downtown Houston on Main Street. The theater was packed and most of those there were African-Americans. At one point towards the end of the movie, Poitier makes the point to Steiger, the sheriff, that Sam Wood could not have been the murderer because there was no way he could have driven two cars at the same time. At this revelation and after a moment of stunned silence, both on the screen and in the movie theater, a voice not far away from where I was sitting, cried out, "Ah, you see the light!" At which everyone in the theater roared with laughter.

"The preservation of the truth" is the fourth of the Great Ends of the Church as stated in our Book of Order. Sometimes the truth is understood in legal terms. In courtroom testimony, one pledges to "tell the truth, the whole truth, and nothing but the truth." As admirable as that promise may be, it is hardly possible. One's understanding of the truth is circumscribed by one's peculiar perspective, and one's perspective is not only limited, but it may also be flawed.

However, from a faith and theological perspective, the truth is embodied in Jesus Christ, and that truth has to do with the absolute goodness of God and of God's unfailing faithfulness to

22

what God has created and of God's boundless grace and love as seen in Jesus Christ. One biblical text that exemplifies this idea of the truth as well as the light is in the opening verses of the Gospel according to John. "In the beginning was the Word, and the Word was with God and the Word was God. He was in the beginning with God; all things were made through him, and without him was not anything made that was made. In him was life, and the life was the light of all people. The light shines in the darkness, and the darkness has not overcome it" (John 1:1-5).

Embedded on the crest of the old Southern Presbyterian Church are the Latin words, "Lux Lucet in Tenebris" -- "the light shines in the darkness." In the darkness of the world human beings have developed there still shines the light of Jesus Christ, that one who said, "I am the light of the world; whoever follows me will not walk in darkness, but will have the light of life" (John 8:12).

Has that light broken into your life? Have you experienced the grace of God that is like a burden lifted from your shoulders? Have you had that sudden and unmistakable awareness of the presence of God in your life to which someone might have said, like that fellow in the movie theater, "Ah, you see the light!" That kind of eye-opening experience may have happened once, or it may have happened multiple times. To experience the peace of Christ or some unmistakable presence of Christ is not something that makes us better than anyone else. It simply makes us better than we were. We have caught a glimpse of the light. We have caught a glimpse of the truth. We have experienced God's grace. The more attentive we are to the possibility of God's presence, the more likely it is that we may experience the truth of God's amazing grace.

It's not the kind of truth that we take and hide. Nor is it the kind of truth that, once we've experienced it, we revel in it and that's as far as it goes. It's the kind of truth that profoundly transforms us and calls us to reflect that truth, that light, in all that we think, say, and do. It's the kind of truth that beckons us out of our comfort zone to do something we never thought we could do -- go to a Sunday school class, teach a Sunday school class, pray more intentionally and more expectantly, think seriously about what God may be calling us to do in very specific and concrete terms.

This past week Jo Ann and I attended and participated in a continuing education event at Pittsburgh Theological Seminary. One of the things we were challenged by was the notion of asking seriously what God might be calling this church to be and do. While some of us are steeped in the tradition of the Presbyterian Church, we also need to look for new ways in which God might be calling this church to be. Maybe God is calling us to do and be something radically different than we've been and done. Maybe not. In any case, doing things in routine ways will no longer work if we are going to have any kind of influence in this community in the years that lie ahead. In seeking what God is calling us to be and do, we need to be a church of the Spirit -- in the words of Joan Gray, we need to be a sailboat church rather than a rowboat church. We need to be a church that is open to the movement of the Spirit, not simply ones that depends on people rowing and rowing and not getting very far.

The preservation of the truth has to do with proclaiming the gospel for the salvation of humankind. It has to do with the shelter, nurture and spiritual fellowship of the children of God. It has to do with the maintenance of divine worship. It has to do with asking why First Presbyterian Church of Pasadena is here at all. How would you answer that question? Why are we here? That's a basic question which requires a specific, concrete answer. I challenge us all to think about how we would answer that question.

So much depends on what frame of mind we're in. Is our mindset such that our prayers are expectant that God is not only present, but active and involved in our lives? Is our mindset like that which Paul recommends to the Philippians? "Let the same mind be in you that was in Christ Jesus, who, though he was in the form of God, did not regard equality with God as something to be exploited, but emptied himself, taking the form of a slave, being born in human likeness" (Phil. 2:5-7).

It is in emptying ourselves of all that distracts and preoccupies us that we may begin to open ourselves up to the presence of the Spirit. What is God calling us to do? A spirit of humility, a spirit of service, a spirit of openness to new ideas and new ways of doing things, a spirit of grace and acceptance, a spirit of wanting to learn and grow. I recall sitting in University Presbyterian Church in Austin when I was a student at the University. During what might have been considered a passing of the peace, I introduced myself to the elderly gentleman in front of me as a student. The gentleman introduced himself by saying that he, too, was a student. I happened to recognize him as a prominent and highly respected professor in the philosophy department. What struck me was not only how he identified himself, but that he was in worship. He was humble and gracious enough to understand that regardless of his prominence he, like the rest of us, stood in need of God's mercy and grace. That's preserving the truth. None of us ever has a lock on the truth. As a church, we preserve it by owning up to our own humanity and our own need for the light of Christ in the world.

We preserve the truth by being led by the Spirit to follow that light in the same way those wise men followed the light to Bethlehem. We preserve the truth by being open to the Spirit and seriously asking ourselves, What would God have us do? We preserve the truth by pointing, with John the Baptist, to Jesus Christ and saying that "he must increase but (we) must decrease" (John 3:30). We preserve the truth by pointing to him who is the

Way, the Truth, and the Life (John 14:6). We preserve the truth by pointing to him who said that "you shall know the truth and the truth will make you free" (John 8:32).

We preserve the truth by pointing to the one who claims us, forgives us. The words penned by Mary Ann Lathbury over 125 years ago to the hymn following today's Affirmation of Faith capture something of this theme of truth as it relates to Scripture. Initially, it sounds like a Communion hymn, but actually it is not. It has to do with the truth to which Scripture points.

> Break thou the bread of life, dear Lord, to me,
> as thou didst break the loaves beside the sea.
> Beyond the sacred page I seek thee, Lord.
> My spirit pants for thee, O living Word!
>
> Bless thou the truth, dear Lord, now unto me,
> as thou didst bless the bread by Galilee.
> Then shall all bondage cease, all fetters fall.
> And I shall find my peace, my all in all.

When we see that sliver of light that points us to the truth, we find ourselves filled full to overflowing with gratitude and a desire to serve him who is the Light of the world.

Thanks be to God!

Chariots of Fire

II Kings 2:1-12

February 15, 2015

Now when the Lord was about to take Elijah up to heaven by a whirlwind, Elijah and Elisha were on their way from Gilgal. Elijah said to Elisha, "Stay here; for the Lord has sent me as far as Bethel." But Elisha said, "As the Lord lives, and as you yourself live, I will not leave you." So they went down to Bethel. The company of prophets who were in Bethel came out to Elisha, and said to him, "Do you know that today the Lord will take your master away from you?" And he said, "Yes, I know; keep silent."

Elijah said to him, "Elisha, stay here; for the Lord has sent me to Jericho." But he said, "As the Lord lives, and as you yourself live, I will not leave you." So they came to Jericho. The company of prophets who were at Jericho drew near to Elisha, and said to him, "Do you know that that today the Lord will take your master away from you? And he answered, "Yes, I know; be silent."

Then Elijah said to him, "Stay here; for the Lord has sent me to the Jordan." But he said, "As the Lord lives, and as you yourself live, I will not leave you." So the two of them went on. Fifty men of the company of prophets also went, and stood at some distance from them, as they both were standing by the Jordan. Then Elijah took his mantle and rolled it up, and struck the water; the water was parted to the one side and to the other, until the two of them crossed on dry ground.

When they had crossed, Elijah said to Elisha, "Tell me what I may do for you, before I am taken from you." Elisha said, "Please let me inherit double share of your spirit." He responded, "You have asked a hard thing; yet, if you see me as I am being taken from you, it will be granted you; if not, it will not." As they continued walking and talking, a chariot of fire and horses of fire separated the two of them, and Elijah ascended in a whirlwind into heaven. Elisha kept watching and crying out, "Father, father! The chariots of Israel and its horsemen!" But when he could no longer see him, he grasped his own clothes and tore them in two pieces.

The year was 1924, the year of the seventh Olympiad in the modern era. That modern era began in 1896 in Greece, resuming a tradition that had begun more than 700 years before the birth of Christ. The only interruption of the modern Olympics was in 1916 due to World War I. The 1924 summer Olympics would be held in Paris. In a true story that was made into an Oscar-winning movie in 1981, "Chariots of Fire", the account was of the competition between a Scotsman, Eric Liddell, and an Englishman, Harold Abrahams. Liddell was an evangelical Christian who felt compelled to honor the Sabbath and refused to run on Sundays. Abrahams was of Jewish extraction. Their friendly competition led them both to representing Great Britain in the Olympics.

It turns out that Liddell was scheduled to run the 100 meter dash on Sunday. When he refused to run, Abrahams took his place and won the gold medal. The next day Liddell ran the 400 meter run and he, too, won a gold medal. Both victories were considered upsets.

The title of the movie, "Chariots of Fire," came from a poem by William Blake who wrote the poem" Jerusalem" in the early 1800s. The line is found in the stanza that reads:

> Bring me my Bow of burning gold:
> Bring me my arrows of desire:
> Bring me my Spear: O clouds unfold!
> Bring my Chariot of fire!

And the next stanza is this:

I will not cease from Mental Fight,
Nor shall my sword sleep in my hand:
Till we have built Jerusalem,
In England's green & pleasant Land.

But Blake's line about his "Chariot of fire", of course, comes from the account we read this morning from II Kings. The prophet Elijah is about to depart this earth, and his successor Elisha pursues him from Gilgal to Bethel to the Jordan, all significant places in Israel's story. In response to Elijah's question as to what Elisha wishes from him before he leaves, Elisha finally asks for "a double share of your spirit" (2:9). Elijah responds, "You have asked a hard thing; yet, if you see me as I am being taken from you, it shall be so for you; but if you do not see me, it shall not be so." And as the two were talking, we are told, "a chariot of fire and horses of fire separated the two of them. And Elijah went up by a whirlwind into heaven. And Elisha saw it..." (2:11-12a).

On this Sunday when we also read of Jesus 'transfiguration experience on a mountain along with Peter, James, and John, we recall that in that experience the disciples see Jesus with Moses and Elijah, representing the Law and the prophets.

It seems that, in asking for a double portion of Elijah's spirit, Elisha is asking for the passion and commitment and faith that Elijah had exhibited. You recall that it was Elijah who confronted the prophets of Baal on Mount Carmel, challenging their gods with the God of Israel. You may recall, however, that it was also Elijah who, in running for his life afterwards, hides – exhausted – in a cave and feared that God had abandoned him. Passion, commitment, and faith are not without their moments of doubt and uncertainty and exhaustion.

On the Mount of Transfiguration Peter, in witnessing Jesus with Moses and Elijah, out of fear and not sure exactly what to do , decides it would be a good idea to construct for each of them a booth as if that would somehow honor them. It's almost as if Peter is so moved and so impressed that he doesn't know what to do, so he thinks he'll build something that would highlight them and that for which they are remembered. After all, doing something is better than doing nothing, right? Not always. His passion is admirable and, no doubt, his heart is in the right place, but somehow he misses the mark.

Sometimes passion and commitment and enthusiasm, like Peter's, miss the mark. We tend to think that bigger is better, more is better, nothing but the gold medal will suffice. Eric Liddell loved to run, and he and Harold Abrahams were united in their desire to win the gold medal. Athletes strive for nothing less. That's the goal, and it's a worthy one. While it is not likely to happen in today's world, Liddell's refusal to run on a Sunday, out of religious convictions demonstrated that, for him at least, there was a higher passion, a higher commitment.

In 1965 Sandy Koufax, the ace pitcher for the Los Angeles Dodgers, refused to pitch the first game of the World Series because it fell on Yom Kippur, a Jewish holy day. When Don Drysdale pitched instead and gave up seven runs in 2 2/3 innings, Drysdale cracked to manager Walter Alston, "I bet you wish I were Jewish today." In 1934 Hank Greenberg, the slugger for the Detroit Tigers, struggled as to whether or not to play in a critical game against the New York Yankees because that day was Rosh Hashanah, another important Jewish holiday. He decided to go ahead and play, and the Tigers won, 2-1, but he struggled with the issue.

But let's take the issue of passion for, and commitment to a higher ideal to another, less noticeable scene. I doubt that very many of us have heard of the name Favio Chavez. His passion for music is profound, and he has a powerful desire to engage young people through music. He lives in Paraguay where many of the people are quite poor. Not to be defeated, he and those young people who are interested in learning music go through trash and find material from which they craft instruments. On a YouTube video, one can listen to them play pieces by Mozart. It's an amazing story.

"Ask what I shall do for you, before I am taken from you," Elijah asks Elisha. "I pray you, let me inherit a double share of your spirit," Elisha responds. How many of us have not, at one time or another, wished we could have the qualities of someone else whom we have admired? In our Walter Mitty-like imaginations, we'd like to think we could play basketball like James Hardin or run like Eric Liddell or pitch like Nolan Ryan or tell stories like Mark Twain or write like Flannery O'Connor or preach like Peter on that first Pentecost or play the cello like Pablo Casals or the violin like Jascha Heifitz.

But as remarkable as those persons are, God made us who we are, and we are given our own gifts which we cultivate with hard work and passion and conviction to the glory of God. The image of "chariots of fire" is an image of doing something important and worthwhile with enthusiasm and conviction. It may be something different for each of us. And anything we do with that spirit will require hard work and we may encounter frustration. Often we see the work of others when they are at their peak. We don't see the number of times they may have fallen short, if not failed altogether. We don't see them in Elijah's cave where he felt like God had abandoned him.

The same is true for the church as well. We may long for the days like the 1950s when churches seemed to be bursting at the seams, but they had their problems too. Those days may not have been as we sometimes like to think. Like it or not, we are not in the 1950s. Our issues and challenges are different, and we need to confront and deal with them with the same kind of energy, intelligence, imagination, love, faith, enthusiasm, and conviction as others faced their challenges. What has not changed is the faithfulness and presence of God and the grace and Lordship of Jesus Christ. We need to submit ourselves to his Spirit now as much as others have in their time.

As we move into God's future, we do so trusting that God's Spirit is leading us, perhaps in ways we would never imagine, but we move forward like "chariots of fire", with joyful abandon and with faith and with hope and with love and with openness to wherever the Spirit leads. We have to do our part, but it does not all fall on us. Trust the Spirit.

Once again, we gather around this table to be fed, so that we can continue our journey with hope and faith and love. We gather where those before us have gathered. We gather here, trusting that the Spirit of Jesus Christ will so inspire and lead us as it has others. We come here ready to be changed, transformed, transfigured if need be, so that God's will may be done.

Thanks be to God!

Wisdom Is Trusting the Catcher

I Kings 2:10-12; 3:3-14

August 16, 2015

Then David slept with his ancestors, and was buried in the city of David. The time that David reigned over Israel was forty years; he reigned seven years in Hebron, and thirty-three years in Jerusalem. So Solomon sat on the throne of his father David; and his kingdom was firmly established....

Solomon loved the Lord, walking in the statutes of his father David; only, he sacrificed and offered incense at the high places. The king went to Gibeon to sacrifice there, for that was the principal high place; Solomon used to offer a thousand burnt offerings on that altar. At Gibeon the Lord appeared to Solomon in a dream by night; and God said, "Ask what I should give you." And Solomon said, "You have shown great and steadfast love to your servant my father David, because he walked before you in faithfulness, in righteousness, and in uprightness of heart toward you; and you have kept for him this great and steadfast love, and have given him a son to sit on his throne today. And now, O Lord my God, you have made your servant king in place of my father David, although I am only a little child; I do not know how to go out or come in. And your servant is in the midst of the people, so numerous they cannot be numbered or counted. Give your servant therefore an understanding mind to govern your people, able to discern between good and evil; for who can govern this your great people?"

It pleased the Lord that Solomon had asked this. God said to him, "Because you have asked this, and have not asked for yourself long life or riches, or for the life of your enemies, but have asked for yourself understanding to discern what is right, I now do according to your word. Indeed I give you a wise and discerning mind; no one like you has been before you and no one like you shall arise after you. I give you also what you have not asked, both riches and honor all your life; no other king shall compare with you. If you will walk in my ways, keeping my statutes and my commandments, as your father David walked, then I will lengthen your life."

"Give your servant an understanding mind to govern your people, able to discern between good and evil" (I Kings 3:9). Such is the prayer of the newly crowned king of Israel, Solomon, successor to King David. Grant me wisdom to govern your people, for who can govern them? No doubt, such is, or should be, the prayer of every person elected president of the United States -- Grant me wisdom to govern your people, for who can govern them? And God is pleased with Solomon's prayer, for he did not ask for long life or riches or defeat of his enemies, but rather he asked for wisdom.

While it might be interesting to examine this passage from the point of view of rulers or political leaders, I am much more interested in the notion of wisdom, in general, and how we understand it. The wisdom of King Solomon was legendary. The book of Proverbs is attributed to him. Immediately following the passage we read this morning is the story of how he resolved the argument between two women, each of whom claimed to be the mother of an infant son. He took the baby boy and said he would settle the dispute by cutting the baby in half and give each of the women half the baby. When the one woman objected and said, No, let the other woman have him, but do not harm the child, Solomon immediately knew who the real mother was.

So, how would you describe, define, or characterize wisdom? What is it that makes a person wise? Clearly, knowledge alone doesn't make someone wise. There are lots of smart and knowledgeable people in the world who show little signs of wisdom. On the other hand, there are lots of persons who may not have much education, but who are wiser than all the Ph.D.s in the world.

One dictionary definition of wisdom is the quality of experience, knowledge, and good judgment. While that might be true, it kind of begs the question, though, doesn't it? Who decides what good judgment is?

In Proverbs we find that "The fear of the Lord is the beginning of wisdom." So maybe, at least from a faith perspective, it has something to do with acknowledging not only that God is far greater than we are or ever could be, but also that before the God who created each one of us and loves each one of us we are to be reverent and humble.

But I think the wisdom that Solomon demonstrated and the wisdom that Scripture refers to goes beyond even that. It's not simply that God is greater than we are. Nor is it simply that we are to be reverent, respectful, and humble before this God. We depend on this God for life. Furthermore, this God has so loved what God has created that God entered this world in the person of Jesus Christ. This God desires to be in relationship with what God has created, and that includes you and me.

In spite of our delusion that we are our own person, in spite of our misguided notion that we are independent and self-reliant and don't need the help of others, the fact of the matter is that we are completely dependent on God -- for life, health, food, clothes, the ability to work. And so, part of what wisdom means is recognition of this.

From today's sermon title one might conclude that I had baseball in mind and the relationship between the pitcher and the catcher, that somehow in order to be an effective pitcher he must trust the knowledge and ability of the catcher. I think that's true, but that's not at all what I had in mind in coming up with the title.

Lately I've been reading a biography of Henri Nouwen, that 20th century Dutch Roman Catholic priest who has had an enormous influence on western Christian spirituality. Apparently, Nouwen was fascinated by circuses. And most particularly, he was taken with the flying trapeze. One of his observations was that the trapeze artists had to be "totally present to the present." They could not let their minds wander or their concentration be diverted. They needed to be fully present to their immediate situation. For them it could be, quite literally, a matter of life and death. The words we read this morning from Jesus' Sermon on the Mount said something about that, did they not? How can we add an hour to a life by worrying or being anxious about something over which we have no control? Be present to the present, and let tomorrow take care of itself.

A second observation that Nouwen made of these flying trapeze artists, and this speaks to the notion of wisdom, I think, is that "the star was not the flyer -- the figure who soars through the air and trusts -- but the catcher whose hands are always there to receive and welcome the flyer home. In a film Nouwen made on his "trapeze theology" Nouwen said, "I can only fly freely when I know there is a catcher to catch me. If we are to take risks, to be free, in the air, in life, we have to know there's a catcher. We have to know that when we come down from it all, we're going to be caught, we're going to be safe. The great hero," Nouwen says, "is the least visible. Trust the catcher" (Wounded Prophet, p. 22).

Trust the catcher. I recall being at Mo-Ranch when I was a child before I knew how to swim. We were in the swimming pool there and my father was treading water in the deep end below the high dive. I stood up there poised to jump. Before I took that leap, I had to trust that Dad was going to catch me. I suspect that, either as children or as parents, we've all had that experience. The leap is a leap of faith and trust. Like the one trapeze artist swinging through the air on the trapeze, we need to learn to trust the catcher, that one who is least visible, but without whom we are doomed.

Solomon's wisdom lay, in part, in his understanding that both as an individual and as ruler over Israel he was subject to and dependent on the wisdom and authority and grace of the God who fashioned and made him and all that is. His wisdom lay in trusting that God was not only there, but would give him what was needed in order to rule wisely and compassionately.

Is that not what we are about when we gather here for worship? We come acknowledging our own need, our own hunger, our own dependence on God for strength and hope and love. We come home – here – where we are reminded that we will be caught by the catcher. We come here to be fed by him who is the bread of life. We come here where we find that one who is, as the hymn says, the "immortal, invisible, God only wise; in light inaccessible hid from eyes." We come here, as the hymn we will sing in a few moments, says, "No one is a stranger here; everyone belongs. Finding our forgiveness here, we in turn forgive all wrongs. We are now a family, of which the Lord is head. Though unseen, he meets us here in the breaking of the bread" ("We Gather Here in Jesus 'Name").

For us, wisdom is acknowledging both who we are and who we are not. We are not God, but we are God's; we belong to God. For us, wisdom is humility as we go about our lives – humility in what we think, in what we say, in what we do. It is knowing that, as Dietrich Bonhoeffer wrote in his book, *Ethics*, we never have the final word on anything; that word always belongs to God. Ours is only the penultimate word. God has the ultimate word.

Wisdom is knowing that we cannot live in the past and we cannot live in the future. It is focusing on the here and now and thanking God for that. For us, however, wisdom is also living with trust in the catcher, trust that as we take risks in all relationships, regardless how they turn out, we will be caught. It is trusting that we will be fed by him who is the bread of life, that we need not hoard, but can trust that God will give us our daily bread -- bread for our body, but, more importantly, bread for our soul and spirit.

Thanks be to God!

Home

Psalm 84

August 23, 2015

How lovely is your dwelling place, O Lord of hosts!
My soul longs, indeed it faints for the courts of the Lord;
My heart and my flesh sing for joy to the living God.

Even the sparrow finds a home, and the swallow a nest for herself,
where she may lay her young, at your altars, O Lord of hosts,
My King and my God.
Happy are those who live in your house, ever singing your praise.

Happy are those whose strength is in you,
In whose heart are the highways to Zion.
As they go through the valley of Baca they make it a place of springs;
The early rain also covers it with pools.
They go from strength to strength; the God of gods will be seen in Zion.

O Lord God of hosts, hear my prayer;
Give ear, O God of Jacob!

Behold our shield, O God;
Look on the face of your anointed.

For a day in your courts is better than a thousand elsewhere.
I would rather be a doorkeeper in the house of my God
than live in the tents of wickedness.
For the Lord God is a sun and shield;
he bestows favor and honor.
No good thing does the Lord withhold from those who walk uprightly.
O Lord of hosts, happy is everyone who trusts in you.

There can be a gravitational pull to this place. Sometimes it's a mid-week visit that draws a person who simply needs to go into the sanctuary and sit, think, and pray. Sometimes a person is drawn here who needs an ear to bend or who, quite frankly, needs financial help of some kind. And sometimes people show up on a Sunday morning without any particular agenda, instinctively needing to be here. We don't know what goes on inside a person, be they members who attend regularly or strangers who happen to show up. We are simply to welcome one and all.

We all know that the church is more than the "bricks and mortar" out of which a building is fashioned. The church is the people. And indeed it is. But the church is more than even the people, is it not? Doesn't the church have to do with the spiritual life of the people? Doesn't the church have something to do with our relationship with God? Isn't the church that place, that body of believers that cultivates, perhaps over a lifetime, our relationship with God, encouraging us to explore, ask questions, find solace at different times in our lives? Recently someone told me that they would not be in worship for awhile as they were discouraged and had to work through some painful issues. While I understood, I also thought that it was too bad because isn't this precisely the place that we are free to confront God with whatever questions, issues, crises that we must confront?

"How lovely is your dwelling place, O Lord of hosts! My soul longs, indeed it faints for the courts of the Lord; my heart and my flesh sing for joy to the living God" (Psalm 84:1-2). This psalm is one which sees the temple in Jerusalem not only as the dwelling place of God, but also as the gathering place of the faithful. There is nothing but good there. Even the sparrow has a place there. It is a place of worship. It is a place of respite. It is a place of safety. It is a place of prayer. A day there is better than a thousand anywhere else, the psalmist says. In short, for the psalmist the temple is home, that place where one is free to be oneself without fear or anxiety, where one is clear about oneself and about one's relationship with this God who is, as we read in another psalm, "merciful and gracious, slow to anger and abounding in steadfast love." That place might be a glorious Gothic cathedral which reflects the majesty and glory of God and, by comparison, the smallness of human beings, or it might be a one-room church house out in the country in mid-America.

But whichever it is and as much as we may admire, love, and feel at home in the place of worship, eventually we must leave. But in leaving, we know we take that home with us. Or, to put it another way, God is not limited to any temple, cathedral, or simple church building, but always goes before us. This place and everything that goes with it shapes who we are and what we believe and how we live.

Last Sunday I read that one of the more articulate spokespersons and activists in the civil rights movement, Julian Bond, died. We included his name in our pastoral prayers. Well, this past week I learned of another person who was described as a "forgotten hero of the civil rights movement." I want to share this with you because I happen to think that the issue of race in this country is one of the most persistent issues that has plagued this country and has gone unresolved.

Jonathan Daniels was a white male, born in March 1939 in Keene, New Hampshire. He had deep roots in New England. In many ways he was typical: he went to music camp, attended church, fell in love, and enjoyed a circle of close friends. He was by no means perfect. He was known to smoke, stay out late, and sneak an occasional beer. But Jonathan had a serious and thoughtful side to him. After high school he attended the Virginia Military Institute in Lexington, Virginia where he thrived under the rigorous academic and physical discipline there. Not knowing what he wanted to do after he graduated, he decided to go to Harvard and pursue a graduate degree in English. After a year there, he decided that that was not for him.

And then he had an epiphany. He never shared what he experienced during the 1962 Easter Sunday services at the Church of the Advent on Beacon Hill, but it changed his life forever. He later called it a "reconversion." After an on-again/off-again relationship with the church, he decided he had come home (there's that word again). Within a year he was enrolled in seminary at the Episcopal Theological School in Cambridge, Massachusetts.

In March 1965 Dr. Martin Luther King, Jr. called on American clergy for assistance after the brutal attack on activists at the Edmund Pettus Bridge in Selma, Alabama. At first Jonathan was not sure -- "could I spare the time? Did I want to spare the time? Did He (God) want...?" But after evening chapel he resolved to go south. He joined the march to Montgomery and then, after most of the activists had returned home and the camera crews had packed up, he stayed.

While managing to complete his seminary coursework, he plunged into what he called "living theology": he helped with voter registration, photographed segregated conditions, worked to integrate a church, and lived with local families, usually black families. He also encountered less than friendly locals. On one occasion, he was accused of being an "outside agitator" and asked if he was a "white nigger," he replied that he was.

On August 14, 1965 Jonathan was part of a protest in Fort Deposit, Alabama. He and twenty others were arrested and held in the Lowndes County Jail in Hayneville where he sat for a week in the sweltering heat. They were released on August 20 and quickly tried to get to a safe place. While some of the activists organized rides, Jonathan and a Catholic priest named Richard Morrisroe, along with two local women, 17-year-old Ruby Sales and Joyce Bailey, walked to a local store known to serve blacks and whites.

As Ruby opened the door, a figure from the shadows warned them to get off the property. Then the man raised a shotgun and pulled the trigger. Jonathan pulled Ruby from the line of fire and was hit instead. He was dead before he hit the ground. The gunman shot Father Morrisroe in the back, and then walked over to the county courthouse to call the state police chief and inform him he had just shot two preachers.

At Jonathan's funeral, many of the mourners stood around the grave and sang the anthem of the movement, "We Shall Overcome" -- a final tribute from those who had come to love this son of New England and his integrity, love, and commitment to freedom.

The one who told this story asked why Jonathan's story is so seldom told. He concluded that whenever his story is told, Jonathan's witness to peace and justice is shared. He goes on to say that Jonathan "is still part of the lives he touched and in the life that he graciously saved. Wherever a person stands up with love and compassion and takes a stand against violence and hatred, Jonathan Daniels is still alive."

I tell you this story, in part, to share a powerful tale about a person of whom very few of us have heard. But I also tell this story because it was in an Easter worship service that Jonathan Daniels underwent a "reconversion" and he discovered that he had come home.

For, you see, home is not simply where we feel comfortable, accepted, forgiven, and free to explore and ask questions in faith and of the faith. Home is also being able to live out our faith and convictions, even – or perhaps especially – when we have questions. Home is trusting that the God we worship and to whom we pray and to whom we express our innermost thoughts, doubts, questions, uncertainties is the same God who goes with us and even goes before us as we step out in faith, doing what we think, hope, and believe is right.

Home is being willing to risk ourselves for a cause we believe to be right and consistent with God's will. Ultimately, home is putting our lives in God's hands and trusting, in the words of Julian of Norwich, that in the end all will be well.

"Happy are those whose strength is in you, in whose heart are the highways to Zion. As they go through the valley of Baca they make it a place of springs; the early rain also covers it with pools. They go from strength to strength; the God of gods will be in Zion" (Psalm 84:5-7).

We gather here not because we have to or out of any sense of guilt. We gather here because this is home. This is where we are safe. This is where we are nurtured. This is where we grow spiritually. This is where we learn to know God and discover God's love for and grace towards us. This is where we discover community, working side by side with other believers, seekers, doubters. This is where we learn and practice the gospel.

But, like Jonathan Daniels, we also must leave this place. We don't leave it behind. Rather, we take it with us as we make our own witness to the good news of God's love, mercy, and justice.

Thanks be to God!

On Whom Does Your Shadow Fall?

Acts 5:12-16

October 4, 2015

Now many signs and wonders were done among the people through the apostles. And they were all together in Solomon's Portico. None of the rest dared to join them, but the people held them in high esteem. Yet more than ever believers were added to the Lord, great numbers of both men and women, so that they even carried out the sick into the streets, and laid them on cots and mats, in order that Peter's shadow might fall on some of them as he came by. A great number of people would also gather from the towns around Jerusalem, bringing the sick and those tormented by unclean spirits, and they were all cured.

I don't know if they still do it, but several years ago one of the regular features of the Reader's Digest magazine was something called "My Most Unforgettable Character." Readers were invited to submit stories describing someone who had a peculiar personality or who had had an unusual impact on this person's life. I always thought it would be fun to submit such an article.

Suppose we were to shift the challenge to be something like persons who have helped shape and influence us into who we are today. I suspect that many, if not most of us could come up with individuals or events or writings that influenced us over the years. Some might have had a negative impact, but my guess is that we could also think of many who had a positive influence on us. And for the time being, let's leave out members of our immediate family.

I remember a high school Sunday school teacher in Houston by the name of David Hannah. At the time I wondered why this wonderful Presbyterian elder wanted to teach a class of high school students. Actually, he co-taught the class. I remember a couple of things about those two teachers. The first was that they took us very seriously. They were gentle and gracious, but they took their responsibilities of teaching and working with high schoolers very seriously. The second thing I remember is that both Mr. Hannah and his co-teacher, whose name escapes me, took different sides on this country's policies having to do with the Vietnam war. And yet, they modeled for the rest of us how two persons could strongly differ with each other on a volatile and controversial issue and, at the same time, remain in the same church, work together in common cause on other matters, and exhibit the kind of Christian grace and cooperation Christ calls us to exhibit.

Another illustration. In another city Jo Ann and I had the opportunity to be a part of church high school choir that numbered over 100 voices. The choir director was Mr. Bill Everitt, at the time owner of the Brook Mays music store. I'm still not sure how he did it, but without great fanfare he was able to make singing hymns and anthems both meaningful to a bunch of 9th through 12th graders, many of whom had no other relationship with or exposure to the church. Over the course of 40 years that choir produced albums of sacred music, sang the Christmas portion of Handel's Messiah on Christmas Eve on KRLD radio in Dallas, and took tours across the United States and Canada where we sang in churches almost every night. How influential that experience was on all those who sang in that choir over the years can hardly be measured. In his own quiet, disciplined, and patient way Mr. Everitt and the music we sang exhibited to the rest of us something of the gospel that remains a part of us.

Still a third example. I remember my second-grade teacher whose name was Patricia Rector. What I recall about her is that she taught us that the educational experience could be fun. What a delightful and happy presence she brought to a room full of seven-year-olds! Other teachers had a similar effect on me, teachers who encouraged thought and reflection.

No doubt, you can think of and name persons who have made a positive difference in your life. In the passage we read this morning from Acts we find the Christian movement emerging with increased numbers and strong leadership. Clearly, Peter was one of those early leaders, this one whose many flaws were exposed during Jesus' lifetime but who since Pentecost seems to have matured and grown into a leader in this new movement. We are told that the people held Peter and those around him in high esteem, and more and more believers, both men and women, were added to their number. And then we come across a fascinating observation Luke makes. Many carried their sick to them to be healed. And when it became so crowded, they would lay them in such a way that they hoped "Peter's shadow might fall on some of them as he came by" (Acts 5:15c).

Whose shadow has fallen on you in your lifetime? Maybe it was a one-time-only encounter, or maybe it is a life-long friend. Perhaps it was a writer whose words became important to you. Or maybe it was simply an experience or an event you witnessed or were part of. This past week Jo Ann and I were in a class that read and discussed the life and work of Henri Nouwen. Our world has been expanded as a result of this renewed acquaintance with this remarkable man who taught that we are not what we have nor what we do, nor is it what others think of us that makes us who we are. Rather, it is the fact that each of us is a child of God who is loved by this God that makes us who we are.

We could broaden the perspective even further. On this World Communion Sunday I would suggest that such persons as Mother Teresa, Martin Luther King, Jr., Aung San Suu Kyi (the Myanmar dissident), and Pope Francis have cast long, positive shadows on the rest of the world. We can go back in history and find many who have helped shape who we are today, both as individuals and as a church. Such persons as John Wycliffe, Jan Hus, Rachel Henderlite, among others, have cast their shadows on us. We are covered with shadows, shadows of persons we recognize and shadows of persons who have shaped us but whose names we will never know.

Even today, we have heard, or will hear, the gospel expressed in languages we may not understand -- Spanish, Urdu, French, and Korean. Not only are we reminded of the global village in which we live, but we are also reminded of the world-wide community of faith that the church has become. This past week we received a letter from the pastor of our sister church in Scotland, extending congratulations on our 75th anniversary.

As we gather around this table today, we do so growing in our awareness of the length and depth and width and breadth of the table of our Lord. Here we are surrounded by that great cloud of witnesses whose race is now over and on whose shoulders we stand. But gathered here also are our brothers and sisters in the faith from around the world -- from Egypt and the Sudan, from South Africa and South America, from China and Myanmar. All who claim the title "Christian" join us, or we join them, at the Lord's table. There's something very exciting about that. Regardless of their theology, regardless of their language, regardless of their age, regardless of their nationality, the hymn by John Oxenham, whose real name was William Dunkerly, rings true: "In Christ there is no east or west, in him no south or north, but one great fellowship of love throughout the whole wide earth."

We know that we have benefitted from having walked in the shadow of others, those who have contributed to our own faith development. But we must also now ask, in all humility, "On whom might our shadow fall?" Do we consider our words or our actions and the effect they might have on someone? The grace and gentleness of an attitude can have as much of a memorable influence on a person as anything else. Do we reflect God's kingdom of love and patience and grace? Some days are better than others, aren't they? The good news is that any influence for good anyone may have is governed by the Holy Spirit. It's not something we can control. We are simply to live as God's people. That's what Peter did. That's what others have done – not doing what they thought others wanted to hear, not trying to live up to expectations; simply living as they thought the gospel called them to live.

On this Peacemaking Sunday we join with those who weep and grieve as well as with those who rejoice and live, with those who live in poverty or live in mansions, with those who have plenty to eat and those who have little or nothing to eat, with those who are American, Mexican, Russian, Nigerian, or Brazilian. The Spirit blows where it wills, Jesus says in John's Gospel. May it blow its gospel through us, casting its shadow on us and on others.

Thanks be to God!

"If It Weren't for the Honor of the Thing, ..."

Acts 5:27-42

October 11, 2015

When they had brought them, they had them stand before the council. The high priest questioned them, saying, "We gave you strict orders not to teach in this name, yet here you have filled Jerusalem with your teaching, and you are determined to bring this man's blood on us. But Peter and the apostles answered, "We must obey God rather than any human authority. The God of our ancestors raised up Jesus, whom you had killed by hanging him on a tree. God exalted him at his right hand as Leader and Savior that he might give repentance to Israel and forgiveness of sins. And we are witnesses to these things, and so is the Holy Spirit whom God has given to those who obey him.

When they heard this, they were enraged and wanted to kill them. But a Pharisee in the council named Gamaliel, a teacher of the law, respected by all the people, stood up and ordered the men to be put outside for a short time. Then he said to them, "Fellow Israelites, consider carefully what you propose to do to these men. For some time ago Theudas rose up, claiming to be somebody, and a number of men, about four hundred, joined him; but he was killed, and all who followed him were dispersed and disappeared. After him Judas the Galilean rose up at the time of the census and got people to follow him; he also perished, and all who followed him were scattered. So in the present case, I tell you, keep away from these men and let them alone; because if this plan or this undertaking is of human origin, it will fail; but if it is of God, you will not be able to overthrow them — in that case you may even be found fighting against God.

They were convinced by him, and when they had called in the apostles, they had them flogged. Then they ordered them not to speak in the name of Jesus, and let them go. As they left the council, they rejoiced that they were considered worthy to suffer dishonor for the sake of the name. And every day in the temple and at home they did not cease to teach and proclaim Jesus as the Messiah.

A couple of years ago the Wednesday Noon Brown Bag Study group studied the civil rights movement in this country based on a series of videos that documented that movement. Last month a pastor's study group of which I have been a part for eight or nine years did some reading on the integration effort that took place at Central High School in Little Rock, Arkansas in September 1957. One of the books that I read in preparation for that conversation was by Carlotta Walls LaNier, one of the African American students who was part of "the Little Rock Nine". Another book was by Daisy Bates, head of the NAACP in Arkansas who served as the adult advisor, friend, confidant, and cheerleader for those African American teenagers who had wanted to gain entrance to Central High School.

The accounts of Carlotta Walls, Daisy Bates, and others who have written of their own experiences of that time reveal such affronts as frequent verbal abuse, being spit upon, seeing their parents lose their jobs, having their homes bombed and then being accused of doing it themselves, family members being arrested without any provocation. And one of the agreements between the school district and the students was that these students were not allowed to participate in any extracurricular activities or even attend any of the school's sporting events. Because such fear tactics had their desired effect on some of the students and their families, a few of the Little Rock Nine students withdrew from Central High School. But some, like Carlotta Walls, persevered and, eventually, graduated in 1960.

Carlotta went on to college, attending first Michigan State University and then earning a degree from Colorado State University. She rarely mentioned to anyone that she had been one of the Little Rock Nine. Even her husband did not discover that fact until she told him many years after their children were born. To say that such an experience as she and others endured made them stronger and built character is to minimize the trauma that they underwent. No doubt, those pioneers made it possible for others to follow without having to undergo what they did. For many, they are heroes, though they themselves hardly see themselves as such.

In the passage we read this morning from Acts Peter and some of the other apostles find themselves and others in the early Christian movement under suspicion and under attack by the Jewish authorities. They are brought before the high priest and other leading elders who imprisoned them for teaching and preaching about Jesus in the temple, something many considered to be violations of the Law. Furthermore, and perhaps more importantly, this movement was gaining more and more followers. After Peter and others of the apostles are imprisoned, the prison doors are mysteriously unlocked, and they return to the temple to teach and preach. Assembled again before the high priest and council, Peter reviews for them the story of Jesus 'death and resurrection and how they were witnesses to these events.

The council was ready to kill them, but a Pharisee by the name of Gamaliel, under whom Paul would study, persuaded them to hold off. Suppose these folks happen to be right? If they are not, they will fail, but if they are right, we might find ourselves "fighting against God!" (Acts 5:39). Acknowledging the wisdom of such an approach, the council decided to release these troublemakers, but not before they had them flogged. And then Luke reports that "as they left the council, they rejoiced that they were considered worthy to suffer dishonor for the sake of the name. And every day in the temple and at home they did not cease to teach and proclaim Jesus as the Messiah" (Acts 5:41-42).

"Considered worthy to suffer dishonor for the sake of the name." While some might ask, "Why me, Lord?", Peter and those early followers counted it an honor to suffer for the cause of Jesus Christ. The roll call of the saints, especially in the early church, included many who were executed. Tradition has it that Peter was crucified upside down because he did not think himself worthy to be crucified in the same way Jesus was. The book of Hebrews tells us that some were stoned to death, others were sawn in two, still others died by the sword (Hebrews 11:37). They were, the writer continues, ones "of whom the world was not worthy" (11:38).

There's a story that's attributed to Abraham Lincoln in which he heard of a person being ridden out of town on a rail. According to Lincoln, that man was heard to have said, "If it weren't for the honor of the thing, I would just as soon walk." One could imagine Peter and some of those early apostles saying something similar. "If it weren't for the honor of the thing, ..." But it was for the honor of the thing, and that made it all worthwhile, worth the preaching and teaching, worth the imprisonment, worth the flogging, worth the death that would certainly come.

In the Gospel lesson that was read this morning we heard about the rich young man who ran up to Jesus asking him what he must do to have eternal life. "Follow the commandments," Jesus said. "Oh, I've done that," the young man boldly replied. "Then, go and sell all that you have and give it to the poor," Jesus told him. And while Jesus looked at him and, Mark says, "loved him," the man went away "shocked" because he was a very wealthy man. Matthew says he went away "grieving." Luke says he went away "sad." The conversation with the disciples continues with Jesus saying that it's easier for a camel to go through the eye of a needle than for a rich person to enter the kingdom. "Who, then, can be saved?" the disciples ask. And Jesus says that as long as we depend on God, all things are possible, but it's when we depend on ourselves that we get into trouble. But the conversation continues beyond that. Peter reminds Jesus that he and the others have left everything behind to follow Jesus, and Jesus replies that they will have their own reward, a hundred times what they have in this lifetime.

Little did Peter and the other disciples realize at that time what following Jesus would mean for them. But following Pentecost and the emergence of a movement of which they would assume early leadership, they quickly found out. I wonder if any of them ever wondered what they had gotten into after the imprisonment, the flogging, and other forms of persecution. Clearly, after this particular encounter with Jewish authorities they began to have a clear idea. And their response? "They rejoiced that they were considered worthy to suffer dishonor for the sake of the name."

A few weeks ago I heard a fellow minister say that she did not wear a cross around her neck because it seemed to her that too often people hide behind the cross. That observation caught my attention because most people seem to wear such a cross out of pride in identifying themselves as Christians. But I think this person's comment was a way of suggesting that discipleship involves more than identifying oneself as part of the Christian movement. It involves a willingness and a commitment that go beyond self-identification. It means not so much asking, Why me? as asking, Why not me? It means being clear about what the costs of discipleship are and accepting them. It means trusting that, for better or for worse, God is with you every step of the way. For the church of Jesus Christ, it means trusting that, when things look bleak for the church or when the church seems to shoot itself in the foot, all will be well because we belong to a God who is always faithful. The church is in service to and belongs to him who is the head. We are called to follow the Spirit wherever it may lead. That's what those first apostles did, and they considered themselves fortunate to be considered worthy to suffer dishonor for the sake of the name.

"If it weren't for the honor of the thing," ... perhaps we would all be better off spending our time and effort elsewhere. But the fact of the matter is that God has called us to this life together and to this work, and it is an honor and a joy and a privilege to be part of this movement. It's more than worth it. In my view there's nothing better.

Thanks be to God!

The Silent Truth

John 18:33-38

November 22, 2015

Then Pilate entered the headquarters again, summoned Jesus, and asked him, "Are you the King of the Jews?" Jesus answered, "Do you ask this on your own, or did others tell you about me?" Pilate replied, "I am not a Jew, am I? Your own nation and the chief priests have handed you over to me. What have you done?" Jesus answered, "My kingdom is not from this world. If my kingdom were from this world, my followers would be fighting to keep me from being handed over to the Jews. But as it is, my kingdom is not from here." Pilate asked him, "So you are a king?" Jesus answered, "You say that I am a king. For this I was born, and for this I came into the world, to testify to the truth. Everyone who belongs to the truth listens to my voice." Pilate asked him, "What is truth?"

On this Christ the King Sunday, the last Sunday in the liturgical year, the Gospel lesson is a familiar one. It is Jesus 'appearance before Pilate. While all four Gospels include the scene of Jesus being brought to Pilate, only John records this conversation. It's almost like a scene in a play. Listen to how J. B. Phillips renders this exchange.

Pilate (to Jesus): Are you the King of the Jews?

Jesus: Are you asking this of your own accord, or have other people spoken to you about me?

Pilate: Do you think I am a Jew? It's your people and your chief priests who handed you over to me. What have you done, anyway?

Jesus: My kingdom is not founded in this world – if it were, my servants would have fought to prevent my being handed over to the Jews. But in fact my kingdom is not founded on all this!

Pilate: So you are a king, are you?

Jesus: Indeed, I am a king. The reason for my birth and the reason for my coming into the world is to witness to the Truth. Everyone who loves truth recognizes my voice.

Pilate: What is truth?

What a strange way to end this conversation! While asking a profound question, Pilate asks Jesus the same question many of us might ask -- what is truth? And yet, the question begs for more conversation, for more of an explanation. It's kind of like asking, what is hope? or what is life? Those kinds of questions defy simple answers.

When a person takes an oath in a courtroom to tell the truth, the whole truth, and nothing but the truth, that person promises that, as far as he or she knows, everything he or she is about to say is accurate. I recall being struck and helped immensely by a statement one of my seminary professors once made when he observed, "There's a difference between truth and accuracy." How would you respond to that statement? Part of what he was saying is that some of the things may or may not be exactly accurate from a historical, biological, or literal point-of-view, but they are true in that they either point to or are part of a larger story. For example, the parables that Jesus tells did not actually happen, so in that sense they are not historically accurate. However, they point to a larger truth about God and God's faithfulness to and love for God's people. Or, is it really important to the larger story whether or not Jonah was actually swallowed by a great fish? Maybe he was, and maybe he wasn't, but to be side-tracked by that issue is to miss the point of the larger story. The same can be said of the creation stories in Genesis. Over against whether the description of creation is literally accurate, what's the larger story?

While Pilate may be interested in determining what kind of crime, if any, Jesus has committed, I think, at least here in John's account, he may be interested in something more, something that we all want but that Jesus does not offer -- at least not in the way we hope or expect. We, like Pontius Pilate, want to figure Jesus out as if he were a puzzle. We, like Pilate, want answers. And so, when Jesus says that he has come into the world to bear witness to the truth, and when he says that everyone who loves the truth recognizes his voice, he seems to be as mysterious as ever.

Frederick Buechner, that wonderful Presbyterian writer, says (in "The Truth of Stories" in *Secrets in the Dark: A Life in Sermons*, pp. 131-137) that the clue lies in the fact that Jesus himself is the truth – as Jesus says elsewhere in John's Gospel. According to Buechner, the kind of truth Jesus is talking about is not something that can be scrutinized, analyzed, and explained as if one were in a court of law. No, Jesus embodies the truth about which he is silent before Pilate. He bears witness to and embodies the truth in the stories he tells, in the way he goes about dealing with people -- from the least reputable to the highest Roman ruler in the land -- in his teachings, in his healing touch.

How do you tell the local Roman ruler that you are a king, but not in the same way that Caesar is king, or emperor? How do you tell or show him that your kingdom is not a political one, like his is, but is quite different? How do you do that in a way that the ruler might understand? Buechner says that no words can contain or explain the truth that Jesus embodies. Therefore, Pilate's question is met with silence -- at least as John reports it.

And do we not often find ourselves in the same boat as Pilate? We want to know what a certain passage means. We want to explain it. We want to know the point. We want to know if this is "going to be on the test." Of course, one of the fascinating things about the stories in Scripture is not only how different persons find different nuggets of meaning in the same passage, but how we ourselves at different stages in our life discover more and more nuances and meanings in a particular passage. I do not read Jesus 'parable of the Prodigal Son today the same way I read it 20, 30, 40 years ago. Not only do I read it differently now, but others have helped me see things I never would have seen on my own.

The same can be said about other texts in the Bible, Old and New Testament. No one meaning captures it all – unless we say that they all point to the mystery of God's incomprehensible love for, and faithfulness to, God's people. And Jesus embodies that love and faithfulness. Gabriel Marcel's observation that "music at times is more like perfume than mathematics" is another way of describing this idea of Jesus as the truth.

In the stories he tells Jesus embodies the truth. Whether it's the parable of the mustard seed or the story of the Good Samaritan or that of the Prodigal Son or the story of the laborers in the vineyard, Jesus is describing the truth. He's describing what the kingdom of God is like, and he embodies that kingdom. He is the truth and, as he says elsewhere in John's Gospel, when we know the truth, the truth will make us free (John 8:32). And that freedom is more than the political freedom many of us think of. It's more than freedom from illness, pain, frustration. It's the kind of freedom that enables us to know joy regardless of our own circumstances.

The truth Jesus is talking about with Pilate is that which is lived and not explained. Somehow, the more one talks about it, the less clear it is. Let me quote Buechner again: "Only Jesus himself is the truth, the whole story of him. He will not let us settle for any truth less than that, tidier than that, easier than that. And the truth seems to be that if he is indeed everybody's best friend the way the old Jesus hymns proclaim, he is at the same time everybody's worst enemy. He is the enemy, at least, of everything in us that keeps us from giving him what he is really after. And what he is really after is our heart's blood, our treasure, our selves themselves. It is the cross he is inviting us to, not a Sunday school picnic, and therefore if it is proper to rejoice in his presence, it is proper also to be scared stiff in his presence" ("The Truth of Stories", p. 136). So writes Frederick Buechner.

Ultimately, Jesus' kingdom will overcome Pilate's kingdom, as John of Patmos has the voices in heaven proclaim in the book of Revelation: "'The kingdom of the world has become the kingdom of our Lord and of his Christ, and he will reign forever and ever" (Rev. 11:15). In the meantime we live as representatives of his kingdom in this world, seeking in a world filled with fear, violence, anger, and death to offer life and hope in the name of him who said, "But take courage; I have overcome the world" (John 16:33). To accept that word is an act of faith. While it's a mystery that can and should be explored, it's useless to try to explain it. It's the silence of truth.

Thanks be to God!

The Runt of the Litter

Micah 5:2-5a

December 20, 2015

But you, O Bethlehem of Ephrathah, who are one of the little clans of Judah, from you shall come forth for me one who is to rule in Israel, whose origin is from of old, from ancient days. Therefore he shall give them up until the time when she who is in labor has brought forth; then the rest of his kindred shall return to the people of Israel. And he shall stand and feed his flock in the strength of the Lord, in the majesty of the name of the Lord his God. And they shall live secure, for now he shall be great to the ends of the earth; and he shall be the one of peace.

When I was growing up, first in Dallas and then in Houston, our family had a dog. Belinda was her name. She was actually a little bit younger than I was, a fact of which I took great note because that meant, as the youngest child of five, I was no longer the baby of the family. Belinda was. When I asked Dad what kind of dog she was, he simply shook his head and said she was a mutt. To this day I still don't know what kind of dog she was, only that she was not one that was greatly appreciated by my father. He tolerated her. In my imagination Belinda was probably the runt of the litter. Evidently, some family came by our house in Dallas asking if we wanted a dog and, for whatever reason – probably my siblings begged and pleaded with my parents and in a moment of weakness – we had a pet that would stay with us until she died around the age of 15 years.

When we were in New York City recently, we saw in Central Park a little Scottie dog sitting in front of a gentleman we presumed to be its owner. I don't know if this dog was the runt of the litter, but we were struck by its patient attentiveness to this gentleman playing Christmas tunes on his saxophone. While we watched and listened, aside from turning his head occasionally, that dog sat still and watched its owner and seemed to be listening.

"But you, O Bethlehem of Ephrathah, who are one of the little clans of Judah, from you shall come forth for me one who is to rule in Israel, whose origin is from of old, from ancient days" (Micah 5:2). The prophet Micah lived in the southern kingdom of Judah and watched as the northern kingdom of Israel was attacked and taken captive by Assyria to the north. He preached warnings to Jerusalem and the rest of the kingdom. This one who told Judah what the Lord requires of humanity, namely, to do justly, to love mercy, and to walk humbly with your God, also prophesied that the tiny little town of Bethlehem, about six miles south of Jerusalem, would be the site chosen by God to enter into this world. Bethlehem, the burial site of Jacob's wife Rachel, and the place where Samuel anointed David king of Israel about 300 years before Micah lived, would become the birthplace of the Savior of the world.

While not the runt of the litter, Bethlehem is not exactly the site most would have thought to be the birthplace of the Messiah. Wouldn't it have made much more sense for Jerusalem, the capital city, the site of the temple, the central place of worship to be the birthplace of the Christ child? Certainly, the Magi seemed to think so as they went there first. But instead, it was Bethlehem of Ephrathah, "one of the little clans of Judah". How very strange.

It almost seems that God goes out of the way to choose the least likely place and the least likely persons to do whatever it is that God wants to do. Virtually everything that God does in this red thread of relationships with human beings throughout Scripture is strange and unexpected. In this season of Advent we note Micah's prophecy of Bethlehem as the home town of a future ruler of Israel. In the passage that was read from Luke we find Mary, whose family was certainly not among the elite, whether politically, socially, or economically, being the chosen one by God to bear the Christ child, and her cousin, Elizabeth, the mother of John the Baptist, came from no higher class than Mary did. And even when in John's Gospel Jesus' first disciples were being gathered and Philip says to Nathanael that he has found the Messiah who happens to have come out of Nazareth, and Nathanael's response is, "Can anything good come out of Nazareth?" (John 1:46).

It's interesting, is it not, that in this season of Advent as we approach the celebration of Christ's birth, in this country at least, we focus on the big and the boisterous and the most eye-catching. In the midst of lovely Christmas lights some of us almost stumble across several persons wrapped in blankets along downtown sidewalks. That is not intended to be a depressing thought. Rather, it's intended to turn our thoughts to the overlooked, the ignored, the outsider, the one whose dear family member just died, the one who is wrestling with depression or some kind of addiction. Do not those kinds of thoughts make the news of God's incarnation in Jesus Christ even more powerful and meaningful, that God has come not as one only for the powerful and the prestigious, but for the likes of you and me? He came for the runt of the litter as much as for the pick of the litter.

This is the very one of whom the prophet Isaiah said, "For he grew up before him like a young plant, and like a root out of dry ground; he had no form or majesty that we should look at him, nothing in his appearance that we should desire him. He was despised and rejected by others; a man of suffering and acquainted with grief; and as one from whom others hide their faces he was despised, and we held him of no account" (Isaiah 53:2-3).

While this is a joyous season, it is so not because of what we make it nor because we can leave our troubles behind, if only for a little while, but rather it is a joyous time because God has deigned to enter this troubled world – not to fix what we have messed up, and not to gloss over "the troubles of the world", as if they can be shoved aside for three to four weeks. God has entered this world to enter our world.

In the play "The Curious Incident of the Dog in the Night-Time" Christopher Boone is a 15-year-old who has Asperger syndrome, high-functioning autism, or savant syndrome. What's fascinating is that the play isn't really about autism so much as it is about Christopher as an outsider, as one who struggles with the world and the world with him. The slightest stimulus, even the human touch, let alone the frenetic noise and movement of a train station, can cause Christopher to withdraw into himself even more. Sioban is a para-professional and mentor at his school. She helps him understand and cope with the outside world. The play opens with Christopher discovering that his dog has been murdered. The rest of the play revolves around Christopher investigating this crime. He records his discoveries in a book he calls "a mystery novel." His disability ignites fears and obstacles within him that make his investigation rather convoluted and scary. Christopher is in a world within a world. Breaking through both worlds, first the outside world that you and I know and then Christopher's own world, has to be the work of a divine agent. But once done, what joy there is for someone like Christopher.

God became human not simply for persons like Christopher, but God enters our world in the same way that someone like Sioban tries to enter Christopher's world to show compassion and love and grace and understanding and to teach us to do the same. It is almost as if we all were autistic, confined to our own little world and unable to comprehend any world beyond our own. And to show God's love for this world, God must enter our world, and God does so in the person of Jesus Christ. And this love that God shows is one in the words of Robert Capon, that cares for the least, the last, and the lost of any of us. Ironically, the more sophisticated we think we are, the more powerful we think we are, the more self-sufficient we think we are, the less open we are to God's love and grace and faithfulness as they are revealed in Jesus Christ and the less likely we are to experience the kind of breakthrough that enables us to experience them in our own lives.

"But you, O Bethlehem of Ephrathah, who are one of the little clans of Judah, from you shall come forth for me one who is to rule in Israel, whose origin is from of old, from ancient days." Not only will the Christ come from Bethlehem of Ephrathah, "one of the little clans of Judah," but the Christ will come for Bethlehem of Ephrathah and all the little clans, however small, however weak, however powerless, however marginalized. In the words of the angel to those shepherds, who were themselves among the lowest of the low in Israelite culture, "to you is born this day in the city of David a Savior, who is the Messiah, the Lord" (Luke 2:11).

Most of us are certainly not among the lowest of the low, at least in economic or sociological terms. We are not among the outcasts of our society. Most of us don't consider ourselves the runt of the litter. All things considered, we are pretty well off, especially compared to the rest of the world. But is that not perhaps the most dangerous condition of all? Might we not, perhaps more than others, because of our relative contentment, miss out on the true joy of God's breaking through into our world with the good news of God's love and grace? I hope not because that news is aimed at each one of us, regardless of our condition.

The last thing I want to mention has to do with that little Scottie in Central Park. While that musician played his saxophone, that dog's attention seemed to be riveted on him. That's where our attention should be, namely, fixed on the God who dared to come into our world and become one of us in Jesus Christ. The more our focus is fixed on this Jesus, the more likely it is that we will hear his words of grace, love, joy, and acceptance. Then, led by his Spirit, we will be able to share that same news with others, seeing all others as God's creatures as well and as our brothers and sisters.

Thanks be to God!

The Sin of Joylessness

Luke 15:11-32

February 14, 2016

Then Jesus said, "There was a man who had two sons. The younger of them said to his father, 'Father, give me the share of the property that will belong to me.' So he divided his property between them. A few days later the younger son gathered all he had and traveled to a distant country, and there he squandered his property in dissolute living. When he had spent everything, a severe famine took place throughout that country, and he began to be in need. So he went and hired himself out to one of the citizens of that country, who sent him to his fields to feed the pigs. He would gladly have filled himself with the pods that the pigs were eating; and no one gave him anything. But when he came to himself he said, "How many of my father's hired hands have bread enough and to spare, but here I am dying of hunger. I will get up and go to my father, and I will say to him, 'Father, I have sinned against heaven and before you; I am no longer worthy to be called your son; treat me like one of your hired hands.' So he set off and went to his father. But while he was still far off, his father saw him and was filled with compassion; he ran and put his arms around him and kissed him. Then the son said to him, 'Father, I have sinned against heaven and before you. I am no longer worthy to be called your son.' But the father said to his slaves, 'Quickly, bring out a robe – the best one – and put it on him; put a ring on his finger and sandals on his feet. And get the fatted calf and kill it, and let us eat and celebrate; for this son of mine was dead and is alive again; he was lost and is found!' And they began to celebrate.

"Now his elder son was in the field; and when he came and approached the house, he heard music and dancing. He called one of the slaves and asked what was going on. He replied, 'Your brother has come, and your father has killed the fatted calf, because he has got him back safe and sound.' Then he became angry and refused to go in. His father came out and began to plead with him. But he answered his father, 'Listen! For all these years I have

been working like a slave for you, and I have never disobeyed your command; yet you have never given me even a young goat so that I might celebrate with my friends. But when this son of yours came back, who has devoured your property with prostitutes, you killed the fatted calf for him!' Then the father said to him, 'Son, you are always with me, and all that is mine is yours. But we had to celebrate and rejoice, because this brother of yours was dead and has come to life; he was lost and has been found.'"

There are some dates that are imprinted in our brains. Growing up, some of us learned "In 1492 Columbus sailed the ocean blue." 1776 is another year that holds meaning for Americans because of the signing of this country's Declaration of Independence. Most recognize the years 1861-1865 as being the years of this country's civil war. August 1914 signified the outbreak of World War I. December 7, 1941 is a day that, according to Franklin Roosevelt, "will live in infamy" when Pearl Harbor was bombed. For many alive today there are dates that hold significance in our national history that took place in our own lifetime -- November 22, 1963 and September 11, 2001.

I would like to suggest another year that in the history of Christianity is one that should be remembered as being extremely important, and that is the year 664. In Whitby, England there was a church gathering that would decide the direction western Christianity would take. In Britain two important traditions had emerged. On the one side was the tradition of St. John which emphasized the goodness of creation and humanity and was known as Celtic theology. The theologian most associated with this view was Pelagius, one who was later declared a heretic. On the other side was the tradition of St. Peter which emphasized the sinfulness of humanity. The theologian most associated with this view was St. Augustine. At the Synod of Whitby in 664 the bishop declared in favor of St. Peter and St. Augustine. It was Augustine who was behind the declaration of Pelagius as a heretic. Over the years the Celtic view declined, but in the 20th century it has emerged again. But many have tried to merge the two views, finding validity in both.

I mention this date – 664 – and the issue at stake at the Synod of Whitby because, as Presbyterians and as products of western Christianity, we are bearers of the legacy of an emphasis on the doctrine of human sinfulness, a doctrine, someone has said, is the only provable doctrine in the Christian faith. The Celtic view sees humanity as basically good, the Augustinian view sees humanity as inescapably flawed.

As a spiritual descendant of St. Peter, St. Augustine, and John Calvin, I certainly affirm the teaching that we are all flawed and broken human beings in need of repentance and the redemption God offers in Jesus Christ. And yet, I think this emphasis on human depravity – or sinfulness – has been at the expense of the joy of the gospel – especially in American Christianity. We are great at guilt. It is, after all, the gift that keeps on giving. We do it to ourselves. We do it to others. Then there's the New Yorker cartoon that has a person lying on a couch in a psychiatrist's office. Sitting in his chair, the psychiatrist observes, "You should be ashamed of yourself for feeling so guilty." Not a big help.

In this kind of world, where is the joy of the gospel? As has been mentioned before, the Christian notion of joy is not equated with worry-free happiness. Rather, it's living with an abiding hope and trust that, in the midst of everything, God is not only somehow at work but also in the end God's will will be done. To live with constant guilt, to live an unhappy life, to be filled with self-pity, one person has said, is the luxury of false religion. It is to live with a kind of hopelessness that allows one to see what's wrong with everyone and everything and never be open to the possibility that God can be – and is – at work in our messy lives. That's part of the story of Scripture, is it not?

As we move through this season of Lent, the focus of our Sunday morning attention will be on some of the parables of Jesus, specifically, those that call for repentance.

Today we read a story that is familiar to most people, Jesus' parable of the prodigal son. But it's the older brother that draws our attention today. While his younger brother has returned home to a father whose joy knows no bounds because he had no idea what had happened to his younger son after he left home on his own, the older, "more responsible" son will not allow himself to join in the joy. He is living in the luxury of false religion. "Listen!" he says to his father. "For all these years I have been working like a slave for you, and I have never disobeyed your command; yet you have never given me even a young goat so that I might celebrate with my friends. But when this son of yours came back, who has devoured your property with prostitutes, you killed the fatted calf for him!" The resentment and the self-pity ooze out of the older brother in a way that is unmistakable. The father, whose joy over the return of a lost (read "dead") son leads him to throw an elaborate party, is equally grateful for the older son. In both cases, the father takes the initiative in going to his sons. The younger son cannot believe his eyes when he sees his father running towards him. The older son cannot see his father's unconditional love for, and acceptance of, him because of his own self-absorption.

Are we not called to see beyond our own circumstances to the gospel which is true and joyful with or without us, whether things are going swimmingly for us or seemingly against us? It's interesting to me that often it is those whose lives are filled with suffering that are the ones who find themselves able to cope best and who are better able to turn to God and see God's love. Some have said that there's no great virtue in suffering, but I do believe that Paul is both right and helpful when he writes to the Romans that "suffering produces endurance, and endurance produces character, and character produces hope, and hope does not

69

disappoint us, because God's love has been poured into our hearts through the Holy Spirit that has been given to us" (Romans 5:3b-5). Suffering does not mean joylessness. That older son had not suffered at all, and yet he could not comprehend the kind of joy that his father was expressing over the return of a lost son.

In this season of Lent perhaps we need to repent of our joylessness – because when we truly hear, receive, appropriate, and experience the gospel, there can be no other response but joy. Joy comes not with knowing we have enough of anything. It is not counting our blessings and realizing that there are others worse off than we are. It is not looking at the rest of the world and understanding how fortunate we are to live here. It is not thinking we have made on our own whatever and whoever we are. It is not harboring the belief that we cannot think of anything bad we've done, so therefore we have nothing to confess. Joy is not the belief that our relationship with God depends solely, or even principally, on us. Our relationship with God was established long before we were ever conceived. "Lord, you have searched me and known me. You know when I sit down and when I rise up," wrote the psalmist. The poet goes on, "For it was you who formed my inward parts; you knit me together in my mother's womb" (Psalm 139).

Joy is realizing our total dependence on God for life, for the very air that we breathe. Joy is recognizing our own personal and spiritual poverty. It is confessing our own illusions of self-sufficiency. It is acknowledging that at the foot of the cross we have nothing to offer but our empty hands. It is hearing the words of God's unconditional grace: "Hear the good news of the gospel: In Jesus Christ we are forgiven. Thanks be to God!" Joy is finally getting it that we can let go of the paralyzing guilt we continually impose on ourselves or have imposed on us by others, and that we can then move on. It is clinging to the affirmation and belief that, as Julian of Norwich wrote centuries ago, in the end all will be well. Joy is realizing that in Jesus Christ we are invited, right now, to live in his kingdom, reflecting the grace, love, kindness, and justice that he embodied and continues to embody through us.

Is it possible for the Celtic way and the Augustinian way to come together? I would like to think so because both have something important to contribute to our understanding of creation and of our relationship to this God whose grace astounds us every morning and whose unfailing love and faithfulness surround us. In this season of Lent – and not in this season only – may we confess our sin and guilt, let go of it, and, in doing so, discover the refreshing joy and freedom of the gospel that only God can give.

Thanks be to God!

A Courthouse Scene

Jeremiah 2:4-13

August 28, 2016

Hear the word of the Lord, O house of Jacob, and all the families of the house of Israel. Thus says the Lord:

What wrong did your ancestors find in me that they went far from me, and went after worthless things, and became worthless themselves? They did not say, "Where is the Lord who brought us up from the land of Egypt, who led us in the wilderness, in a land of deserts and pits, in a land of drought and deep darkness, in a land that no one passes through, where no one lives?" I brought you into a plentiful land to eat its fruits and its good things. But when you entered you defiled my land, and made my heritage an abomination. The priests did not say, "Where is the Lord?" Those who handle the law did not know me; the rulers transgressed against me; the prophets prophesied by Baal, and went after things that do not profit. Therefore once more I accuse, says the Lord, and I accuse your children's children. Cross to the coasts of Cyprus and look, send to Kedar and examine with care; see if there has ever been such a thing. Has a nation changed its gods even though they are no gods? But my people have changed their glory for something that does not profit. Be appalled, O heavens, at this, be shocked, be utterly desolate, says the Lord, for my people have committed two evils: they have forsaken me, the fountain of living water, and dug out cisterns for themselves, cracked cisterns that can hold no water.

Some people are fascinated with courtroom drama. It might be the fictional stories by Erle Stanley Gardner, author of what became the television series of Perry Mason, or it might be the real life court room drama in trials such as the O. J. Simpson trial. For some, the interest might be in the substance of the issues itself, while for others it's the drama of the attorneys themselves. Percy Foreman and Richard "Racehorse" Haynes were two prominent Texas attorneys who heightened public interest in trials.

A good friend of mine is an expert on the trial of John Scopes in July 1925 in Dayton, Tennessee. In fact, in 1965 my friend interviewed Scopes in Shreveport, Louisiana where Scopes lived in retirement. Subsequently my friend wrote and edited a book about Scopes and the so-called "Monkey Trial". He has continued to return to Dayton over the past 50 years for reunions and to hear papers delivered on one of the most significant trials in this country in the 20th century. The courthouse is still there and, as I understand it, the courtroom is as it was 91 years ago. In that very room Clarence Darrow and William Jennings Bryan squared off against each other, Darrow for the defense and Bryan for the prosecution. I suspect, if one is quiet enough there, one can almost hear their voices.

It is a courtroom scene that I would like for us to imagine this morning -- not necessarily the one in Dayton, Tennessee, but the typical courtroom with a judge sitting on a raised platform with two desks below, one for the prosecution and one for the defense. Behind the railing are chairs for the audience. Whether it's from your own personal experience or from watching courtroom scenes in film or on television, the scene is familiar enough that we can picture it.

Jeremiah uses judicial language, courtroom language in the passage we read this morning. The same kind of imagery can also be found in several places in Isaiah. It's as if in the prophet's eyes God is playing the role of sometimes prosecutor, sometimes judge. Charges are leveled against Judah: "What wrong did your ancestors find in me that they went far from me, and went after worthless things, and became worthless themselves? They did not say, 'Where is the Lord who brought us up from the land of Egypt, who led us in the wilderness, in a land of deserts and pits, in a land of drought and deep darkness, in a land that no one passes through, where no one lives?'"

And then this part of the prosecution's argument concludes: "Be appalled, O heavens, at this, be shocked, be utterly desolate, says the Lord, for my people have committed two evils: they have forsaken me, the fountain of living water, and dug out cisterns for themselves, cracked cisterns that can hold no water." The prosecutor God accuses the people, essentially, of desertion from the one who had so faithfully guided them.

In these judicial scenes in which charges are leveled against the people of God, one might wonder where the defense attorney is. The people have no answer, no excuses. God who has always been faithful to them now finds that they have turned away from God in search for other, more manageable gods, or perhaps they have decided there is no god at all. They have handled the law, the prosecutor says, but not in a way that God intended.

The issues of innocence and guilt are not only important ones in matters of law; there's been a whole industry in the field of psychology that has dealt with guilt. But in matters of faith and theology the issues of guilt and innocence also play an important role because they help define who we are as human beings and, as a result, they inform our relationship with God. Some might say that too much emphasis has been placed on the role of guilt in our lives. Perhaps so, but from a theological perspective, it's place cannot be ignored or minimized.

Jeremiah was confronting the people of Judah with their guilt, their going against the God who had created them and who had seen them through challenges going all the way back to Abraham. It was not so much a matter of shame as it was a matter of confronting them with the fact that for a long time they had taken a wrong turn. Jeremiah, along with other prophets, was calling them to turn around, to remember, in short, to repent and remember who they were and who their God was.

Confronting and confessing our foolishness and wrongdoing does not erase the fact that we are and remain sinners. Confronting and confessing our foolishness and wrongdoing reminds us who we are and whose we are – we belong to a God who loves us, as one of our more recent catechisms puts it. But confessing our foolishness and our shortcomings also opens up the possibility of hearing God's word of grace – that God does not desert us, that God is faithful and patient and gracious, "slow to anger and abounding in steadfast love", as the psalmist puts it. We may still be sinners, but now we are God's forgiven sinners.

Now, let's go back to that courtroom scene. We have noted that there's a prosecutor in the scene, the one bringing charges against the people of Judah. Jeremiah is God's spokesperson there. Through Jeremiah, God is the prosecutor. God must also be the judge. But the good news is that God is also the defense attorney. This God who confronts the people of Judah with their disobedience and guilt is also the God who comes to us in Jesus Christ – Immanuel, God with us. In this courtroom the law is important, but it is the spirit of the law that reigns supreme, not the letter of the law. It's the law of love and mercy and acceptance.

This God – this prosecutor, judge, and defense attorney – is a gracious and forgiving God. God's love and grace are indeed unconditional. It would, however, be cheap grace if we were to hear this good news as a warrant to go on and do what we want to do anyway. Costly grace would be to hear this good news and begin to realize God's claim on us, God's forgiveness of us, God's call to us reflect the high joy and privilege it is to participate in kingdom life, to reflect that same forgiveness, grace, and faithfulness in our lives and in our relationships with others.

That's a challenge in any generation, but it seems particularly challenging in our world, a broken one in which language is abused, people are abused, the environment is abused, relationships are abused. For many, the world is hopelessly broken. Surely, there were people in Judah who had similar sentiments. Ever since King Solomon, Israel was no longer one country, but divided into the northern kingdom of Israel and the southern kingdom of Judah. Then, the Assyrians took the northern kingdom of Israel for itself, leaving only Judah. And now, the Babylonians were assaulting Judah and its capital, Jerusalem, and would soon take it for itself. What kind of future would there be?

And yet, in the midst of being confronted with her own failures and shortcomings, Judah would discover God's mercy and faithfulness. The good news of the gospel is that we do too. Whether it's a personal issue that leaves us devastated or a public issue that leaves us distressed, if not depressed, the God of Israel and Judah, the God of our Lord Jesus Christ remains with us.

If we put our trust in this God whose kingdom has dawned in Jesus Christ, then that trust is well-placed. Things may not go the way we think they should go, but that's all right because we know that we never have the last word. We do the best we can, we live trying to represent Jesus in the world, treating others with love and humility, offering aid where we can, and then kneel at the cross.

Things did not turn out all that great for Jesus, did they? But God took the worst that humankind could give and even then embraced this world with love and offered new life. It's in that courtroom that we will discover God's justice and mercy.

Thanks be to God!

A Broken Spirit

Luke 18:9-14

October 23, 2016

Jesus also told this parable to some who trusted in themselves that they were righteous and regarded others with contempt: "Two men went up to the temple to pray, one a Pharisee and the other a tax collector. The Pharisee, standing by himself, was praying thus, 'God, I thank you that I am not like other people: thieves, rogues, adulterers, or even like this tax collector. I fast twice a week; I give a tenth of all my income.' But the tax collector, standing far off, would not even look up to heaven, but was beating his breast and saying, 'God, be merciful to me, a sinner!'" I tell you, this man went down to his home justified rather than the other; for all who exalt themselves will be humbled, but all who humble themselves will be exalted."

This is a fascinating parable. In fact, at various times in my life it has been one of my favorites, mainly because it serves as a warning against arrogance, hypocrisy and self-righteousness, characteristics that seem to afflict much of what has passed for Christianity in my lifetime. And the parable has forced me to call to mind many who are also of the Christian faith who have exemplified the characteristic of humility – not simply self-effacement but trying to see in others the face of Christ and the value of their point-of-view, even when they may be in sharp disagreement with them. They recognize that they themselves are in as much need of God's grace and mercy as anyone else.

I must confess, however, that this week I have struggled with this parable in a way that I have not before. I have been reading it in light of that powerful line in Psalm 51, "A sacrifice acceptable to God is a broken spirit; a broken and contrite heart,

O God, you will not despise" (Psalm 51:17). If we look at the tax collector in the story Jesus tells, clearly his spirit has been broken. It is left to our imagination to consider what has happened that has driven him to his knees. Is it because as a tax collector he realizes that he has been working for the occupying Roman government or that, in doing so, he, like Zaccheus, knows that he has cheated some of his fellow citizens? Or, is it because someone very close to him has died and he has suddenly realized how fragile life can be? Or, is it because his marriage is in trouble and realizes his responsibility for at least part of it? We don't know and, because Jesus doesn't tell us, maybe it's not all that essential to the parable.

If the tax collector is an example of the psalmist's idea of the "broken spirit" that God desires, clearly the Pharisee is not. He is satisfied with, if not proud of, who he is and what he has become. And why shouldn't he be? He's a good man, a good Pharisee who practices what his tradition has taught what is good and right – he goes to church, he prays, he fasts, he tithes. Perhaps his prayer thanking God that he's not like other people is his way of thanking God for who he is. He's been blessed.

Has his spirit been broken? And exactly what is meant by that?

The problem is that there's another way to understand what a broken spirit is, and most of us would find it objectionable. It's the kind of brokenness that results from harsh words that dash dreams, discourage hopes, and abuse aspirations. It's the kind of brokenness that leaves one feeling limp and without purpose or direction. It's what bullies do.

That may not be the kind of broken spirit that either the psalmist or Jesus has in mind. The kind of brokenness that that tax collector experienced, I suspect, is both painful and necessary. It may be similar to what an alcoholic or a drug addict must experience before he or she is able to surrender to a higher power, namely, God. They say that a person must hit "rock bottom" before he or she becomes convinced that they need help. But when that happens, they are able to admit their own shortcomings and flaws and begin to discover the goodness and grace of God. The focus of attention is not on how good they are or what they can do or have accomplished or even on what brings them pleasure, but on their own humanity and their need for God if there is to be any hope at all of inner peace, strength, wholeness, and spiritual growth.

The words of Jeremiah come to mind when he tells the story of the potter and his clay. Jeremiah is instructed to go to the potter's house. So Jeremiah goes and sees the potter working at his wheel. Jeremiah reports, "The vessel he was making of clay was spoiled in the potter's hand, and he reworked it into another vessel, as seemed good to him" (Jeremiah 18:1-4). The prophet Isaiah uses that same language to talk about the relationship between God and humanity (Isaiah 64:8). But that relationship can only develop and be cultivated if we surrender our broken selves to the only one who can make us whole.

"A sacrifice acceptable to God is a broken spirit; a broken and contrite heart you will not despise." "God, be merciful to me, a sinner." The kind of brokenness that is being described here is one that is open and willing to be molded and shaped into a new creation, one that is willing, as Paul says, to leave the past behind and strain forward to what lies ahead (II Cor, 5:17 and Phil. 3:13-14), knowing and trusting that God goes with and ahead of us.

The hymn we will sing in a few moments was written by John Greenleaf Whittier in 1872. An American Quaker, Whittier wrote this as part of a longer poem called "The Brewing of Soma." Apparently, "soma" is an intoxicating drink used in religious rites of a Hindu sect in India. In the poem Whittier describes the effects of this potion on those who drink it. It is called "the drink of the gods" because it causes those who

consume it to enjoy the illusion that they could become divine.
A few of the lines go like this:

> They drank, and lo! in heart and brain
> A new, glad life began;
> They grew of hair, grew young again,
> The sick man laughed away his pain,
> The crippled leaped and ran.

> "Drink, mortals, what the gods have sent,
> Forget you long annoy."
> So sang the priests, From tent to tent
> The Soma's sacred madness went,
> A storm of drunken joy.

> Then knew each rapt inebriate
> A wing and glorious birth,
> Soared upward, with strange joy elate,
> Beat, with dazed head, Varuna's gate,
> And sobered, sank to earth....

> And yet the past comes round again,
> And new doth old fulfill;
> In sensual transports wild as vain
> We brew in many a Christian fane
> The heathen Soma still!

And then we come to this verse, familiar to most of us:

> Dear Lord and Father of mankind,
> Forgive our foolish ways!
> Reclothe us in our rightful mind,
> In purer lives Thy service find,
> In deeper reverence, praise.

The poem reflects both our brokenness and our penchant for trying to fix ourselves, by trying to manufacture things that will bring us happiness. The poem is a prayer of confession and repentance. The verse that opens the hymn that we know is a plea to God to "reclothe us in our rightful mind", to take our brokenness and make us whole.

Even in praying, fasting, and giving tithes, the Pharisee was, as Jesus put it, trusting only himself and showing contempt for others, while the tax collector was broken and knew it, and was only then able to discover wholeness. We are all capable of the arrogance and self-righteousness of the Pharisee. The truth of the matter is, whether we realize it or not, we are all broken, in one way or another, and we might actually be both the Pharisee and the tax collector. We might be the Pharisee some days when we are unable to see our brokenness and we take great pride and satisfaction in who we are and what we think we have become, and on other days we recognize our brokenness and can only say, "God, be merciful to me, a sinner!"

"A sacrifice acceptable to God is a broken spirit." "God, be merciful to me, a sinner!" "Reclothe us in our rightful mind, in purer lives Thy service find, in deeper reverence, praise." May we discover and admit our brokenness, and, in doing so, may we discover the joy of knowing that we belong to him who was broken for our sakes and who makes us whole, Jesus Christ himself.

Thanks be to God!

The Messiness of Realizing a Vision

Isaiah 35:1-10

December 11, 2016

The wilderness and the dry land shall be glad, the desert shall rejoice and blossom; like the crocus it shall blossom abundantly, and rejoice with joy and singing. The glory of Lebanon shall be given to it, the majesty of Carmel and Sharon. They shall see the glory of the Lord, the majesty of our God.

Strengthen the weak hands, and make firm the feeble knees. Say to those who are of a fearful heart, "Be strong, do not fear! Here is your God. He will come with vengeance, with terrible recompense. He will come and save you."

Then the eyes of the blind shall be opened, and the ears of the deaf unstopped; then the lame shall leap like a deer, and the tongue of the speechless sing for joy. For waters shall break forth in the wilderness, and streams in the desert; the burning sand shall become a pool, and the thirsty ground springs of water; the haunt of jackals shall become a swamp, the grass shall become reeds and rushes.

A highway shall be there, and it shall be called the Holy Way; the unclean shall not travel on it, but it shall be for God's people; no traveler, not even fools, shall go astray. No lion shall be there, nor shall any ravenous beast come up on it; they shall not be found there. And the ransomed of the Lord shall return, and come to Zion with singing; everlasting joy shall be upon their heads; they shall obtain joy and gladness, and sorrow and sighing shall flee away.

Presidential inaugurations are often occasions for presidents to offer a vision for the country. Lincoln's Second Inaugural Address, extraordinarily brief and given on March 4, 1865, submits this vision to a nation torn apart by four years of civil war: "With malice toward none; with charity for all; with firmness in the right, as God gives us to see the right, let us strive on to finish the work we are in; to bind up the nation's wounds; to care for him who shall have borne the battle, and for his widow, and his orphan – to do all which may achieve and cherish a just, and a lasting peace, among ourselves, and with all nations."

Sixty-eight years later when the country was in the midst of another, but much different crisis Franklin Roosevelt offered a vision that included these well-known words: "The only thing we have to fear is fear itself." In that same speech he reminded the citizens of this country of their dependence on each other with these words: "If I read the temper of our people correctly, we now realize as we have never realized before our interdependence on each other; that we cannot merely take but we must give as well; that if we are to go forward, we must move as a trained and loyal army willing to sacrifice for the good of a common discipline, because without such discipline no progress is made, no leadership becomes effective."

Then, of course, John F. Kennedy inspired many with these words from his inaugural speech in January of 1961: "And so, my fellow Americans, ask not what your country can do for you, but what you can do for your country." Martin Luther King's "I Have a Dream" speech in August 1963 lifts up a vision that has inspired, and continues to inspire, many.

Part of the inspiration of a vision is found in the ability of a person to paint a picture of what is desirable but not yet achieved. By the very use of the word "dream" Dr. King was pointing to a vision that was not yet realized, but was certainly to be desired. Included in the vision he evoked in that speech are references to another vision found in Isaiah, namely, "I have a dream that one day every valley shall be exalted, every hill and mountain shall be made low. The rough places will be made plain, and the crooked places will be made straight. And the glory of the Lord shall be revealed, and all flesh shall see it together. This is our hope." The poetic power of his words combined with the picture they painted has inspired persons of all races ever since.

In the passage we read this morning from another chapter in the prophecy of Isaiah we find a vision offered at a time when the northern kingdom of Israel was being taken by the world power at the time, Assyria. This was about 740 years before the birth of Jesus. "Strengthen the weak hands, and make firm the feeble knees. Say to those who are of a fearful heart, 'Be strong, do not fear!'... Then the eyes of the blind shall be opened, and the ears of the deaf unstopped; then the lame shall leap like a deer, and the tongue of the speechless sing for joy. For waters shall break forth in the wilderness, and streams in the desert." And, finally, "And the ransomed of the Lord shall return, and come to Zion with singing; everlasting joy shall be upon their heads; they shall obtain joy and gladness, and sorrow and sighing shall flee away".

Visions can be wonderful. Indeed, one translation of a well-known verse in the book of Proverbs which was quoted in an inaugural speech within our lifetime reads, "Where there is no vision, the people perish" (29:18). The problem with visions, even if everyone finds them noble and inspiring, is making them become real. People may disagree on how to get there. Think about the inspired and inspiring words in the Declaration of Independence: "We hold these truths to be self-evident, that all men are created equal, that they are endowed by their Creator with certain unalienable Rights, that among these are Life, Liberty, and the pursuit of Happiness." Who would disagree with those words written 240 years ago? And yet, look at the struggle we in this country have had in trying to realize that vision -- and we still have a long way to go. Some say we have moved too slowly, others say we have moved too quickly, while still others wonder if we will ever reach any semblance of that vision that includes equality for all people.

If we compare our reading from Matthew this morning with Isaiah's vision that we also read or even with some of the other visions of a hoped-for Messiah that appear later in Isaiah, it becomes clear that nothing is very clear. "Are you the one who is to come, or are we to wait for another?" John's disciples ask Jesus. Through the years the Jews had hoped for a Savior, but how would they know who that would be and when he would appear? Would he come as a military leader, a revolutionary who would re-claim Israel's independence from the Romans? Would he come as a political leader, seeking to undermine the occupying Romans? Would he be a religious leader, seeking the support of the Pharisees, scribes, and Sadducees? Surely he would be one who would rise to prominence in Jerusalem, the site of the temple where all things important for Jews took place.

Our Wednesday Noon Brown Bag Bible Study has been reading and discussing the Gospel according to John in recent weeks. One of the issues that is important for John is for his readers to deal with the question, Who is Jesus, and is he the Messiah? And we have tried to put ourselves in the position of Jesus' contemporaries. How would we have responded to what Jesus said and did? Suppose you had been one of the disciples? Wouldn't you have wondered, as many did, "Is this what the Messiah looks like?" I suspect that some, if not most, of us might have been a bit skeptical. But moving from vision to reality is messy because so often our expectations do not match the realization of that vision. "Are you the one who is to come, or are we to wait for another?"

Then in our Wednesday Bible study group we wondered aloud if we would recognize Jesus if he were to walk through the fellowship hall door. And someone wisely observed that perhaps we would not have to look very far or wait very long. If we look in the face of whoever walks through the door, whether they look like us or not, whether they are rich or poor, well-dressed or nattily dressed, male or female, adult or child, we may very well see the face of Jesus. It may not be what we envisioned Jesus to look like, but there he is.

Advent is a time of waiting, we are told, but dare not wait too long because if we are serving another, then that service may be like waters that break forth in the wilderness, and streams in the desert. And if we find ourselves feeling as if we were in a desert, parched and dry, knowing what it means to feel famished, spiritually, and by the grace of God we are fed and are awakened to new life, then Isaiah's vision will become a reality for us. It may not look like what we expected, but then God seems to be full of surprises -- like showing up in an out-of-the-way country village to two unknown, poor, uninfluential persons with little to commend them than open hearts to the will of God, like challenging many of the customs and laws of the religious leadership of the day, like   siding with those no one else considers worthy of attention -- the blind, the lame, the overweight, the underweight, the long-haired, the short-haired, women (who were considered by most less than men), servants, children. What kind of Messiah is that? Certainly not the kind that most expected.

And yet, ... God is full of surprises. God's vision and our expectations are not always the same. In fact, one might even say that they are rarely the same – in which case all we can do is imagine God's vision as it is expressed through such prophets as Isaiah and then see how it might be realized now. It may seem messy, but it's messy only because of our poor eyesight.

"Say to those who are of a fearful heart, 'Be strong, do not fear! Here is your God.... Then the eyes of the blind shall be opened, and the ears of the deaf unstopped; then the lame shall leap like a deer, and the tongue of the speechless sing for joy. For waters shall break forth in the wilderness, and streams in the desert." Can we see that vision realized in our lives and in this world? No? Maybe we will if we try to see Jesus in ourselves and in those we encounter, whoever they may be. The neat thing is that we don't have to wait until Christmas Day.

Thanks be to God!

The Cradle and the Cross

Luke 2:1-20

December 24, 2016

In those days a decree went out from Emperor Augustus that all the world should be registered. This was the first registration and was taken while Quirinius was governor of Syria. All went to their own towns to be registered. Joseph also went from the town of Nazareth in Galilee to Judea, to the city of David called Bethlehem, because he was descended from the house and family of David. He went to be registered with Mary, to whom he was engaged who was expecting a child. While they were there, the time came for her to deliver her child. And she gave birth to her firstborn son and wrapped him in bands of cloth, and laid him in a manger, because there was no place for them in the inn.

In that region there were shepherds living in the fields, keeping watch over their flock by night. Then an angel of the Lord stood before them, and the glory of the Lord shone around them, and they were terrified. But the angel said to them, "Do not be afraid; for see — I am bringing you good news of great joy for all the people: to you is born this day in the city of David a Savior, who is the Messiah, the Lord. This will be a sign for you: you will find a child wrapped in bands of cloth and lying in a manger." And suddenly there was with the angel a multitude of the heavenly host, praising God and saying, "Glory to God in the highest heaven, and on earth peace among those whom he favors."

When the angels had left them and gone into heaven, the shepherds said to one another, "Let us go now to Bethlehem and see this thing that has taken place, which the Lord has made known to us." So they went with haste and found Mary and Joseph, and the child lying in the manger. When they saw this, they made know what had been told them about this child; and all who heard it were amazed at what the shepherds told them. But Mary treasured all these words and pondered them in her heart. The shepherds returned, glorifying and praising God for all they had heard and seen, as it had been told them.

I have a friend who occasionally asks me what my favorite holiday is. I'm never sure how to answer because each one is different and carries special meaning. Almost without hesitating my friend declares that Christmas is his favorite. I suspect that he is not alone in that sentiment. Apart from the giving and receiving of presents, the festive family get-togethers, the sporting events that many enjoy, apart from all that, the gospel message at Christmas is of a light that shines in the darkness. From Isaiah's "The people who walked in darkness have seen a great light" (Isaiah 9:2) to Matthew's description of the star that guides the wise men in the darkness to John's "The light shines in the darkness, and the darkness did not overcome it" (John 1:5) to Paul's "you are all children of light and children of the day; we are not of the night or of darkness" (I Thessalonians. 5:5), we hear words of hope and light in a world that is dark and depressing to so many.

And what is that message that offers hope and light? One person, poet and novelist Jay Parini, has written that this message is a radical one in that Jesus calls for us to live with love instead of power, humility instead of arrogance, hope instead of fear. Instead of revenge, through Jesus God teaches us to turn the other cheek, to love our enemies, and to practice forgiveness. Instead of judging others, we are called to seek forgiveness for our own shortcomings. Totally against the grain of what we want to do, this message is life-changing, but difficult.

The incarnation – the fact that God freely chose to put on flesh and become a part of the human race – is a reflection not only of Emmanuel, God with us, but also of God for us. What happened in that manger scene over 2000 years ago is the miracle of God showing God's love for and faithfulness to a world that has ignored, if not rejected God. "He came to what was his own, and his own people did not accept him" (John 1:11). And yet, God did not give up on them. Like Francis Thompson's poem "The Hound of Heaven", God pursues us "down the nights and down the days; ...down the arches of the years; ...down the labyrinthine ways of my own mind; and in the mist of tears I hid from Him, and under running laughter".

And so, this scene with the creche and Mary and Joseph and the babe surrounded by sheep and shepherds, wise men and camels, angels and other creatures reflects God's persistent desire to be in relationship with us, God's stubborn refusal to give up on us.

But the story of the gospel does not end with Christmas. It does not even end with Jesus 'teachings of love and forgiveness. The Christmas story is incomplete unless and until Bethlehem and the nativity scene are seen against the backdrop of the empty cross, the cross of Good Friday and Easter. As the anthem "Christmas Communion Song" by John Ray and Susan Callaway puts it, "God clothed in human flesh, Immanuel, From heaven descended, with us to dwell. Once clothed in mystery, hidden, concealed. Truth in a manger, now is revealed. Celebrate His coming, meditate the cost. Look beyond the cradle and behold the cross. Drink the cup of joy, eat the bread of life. Taste and see the beauty of this holy night."

That God not only came into this world but that God became one of us and gave himself up for us, or as Paul puts it, this Christ "emptied himself, taking the form of a slave, being born in human likeness. And being found in human form, he humbled himself and became obedient to the point of death – even death on a cross" (Philippians. 2:7), is a reflection of God's own self-giving and extraordinary compassion, love, and faithfulness.

As we gather around this table, we gather around him who is the light of the world, the one who brings light into this world and into our lives. When we hear the words of the angel, "Do not be afraid; for see – I am bringing you good news of great joy for all the people: to you is born this day in the city of David a Savior, who is the Messiah, the Lord", may we hear them as addressed to us. To us – and for us – is born a Savior who is the Messiah, the Lord.

Lest we feel overwhelmed by the darkness, I want to close with a poem by Ann Weems, that Presbyterian poet who had a firm grasp on the reality of the world in which we live as well as an equally firm grasp on the Christian hope. The poem is entitled "Not Celebrate?" and goes like this:

Not celebrate?
Your burden is too great to bear?
Your loneliness is intensified during this Christmas season?
Your tears seem to have no end?
Not celebrate?
You should lead the celebration!
You should run through the streets
to ring the bells and sing the loudest!
You should fling the tinsel on the tree,
and open your house to your neighbors,
and call them to dance!
For it is you above all others
who know the joy of Advent.
It is unto you that a Savior is born this day,
One who comes to lift your burden from your shoulders,
One who comes to wipe the tears from your eyes.
You are not alone,
for he is born this day to you.

"The light shines in the darkness and the darkness did not overcome it."

Thanks be to God!

A Legacy of Doxology

I Peter 1:3-9

April 23, 2017

Blessed be the God and Father of our Lord Jesus Christ! By his great mercy he has given us a new birth into a living hope through the resurrection of Jesus Christ from the dead, and into an inheritance that is imperishable, undefiled, and unfading, kept in heaven for you, who are being protected by the power of God through faith for a salvation ready to be revealed in the last time. In this you rejoice, even if now for a little while you have had to suffer various trials, so that the genuineness of your faith – being more precious than gold that, though perishable, is tested by fire – may be found to result in praise and glory and honor when Jesus Christ is revealed. Although you have not seen him, you love him; and even though you do not see him now, you believe in him and rejoice with an indescribable and glorious joy, for you are receiving the outcome of your faith, the salvation of your souls.

With less than a year left to live (although, obviously, he did not know that at the time), Dietrich Bonhoeffer penned a letter to his close friend and colleague, Eberhard Bethge. On August 23, 1944 he had already been in the Tegel prison in Berlin for well over a year. This collection of letters is fascinating – not only from the point-of-view of Bonhoeffer as a person, but also from his perspective as a theologian.

But this particular excerpt from that August 23rd letter is telling. He writes: "Please don't ever get anxious or worried about me, but don't forget to pray for me – I'm sure you don't! I am so sure of God's guiding hand that I hope I shall always be kept in that certainty. You must never doubt that I'm traveling with gratitude and cheerfulness along the road where I'm being led.

My past life is brim-ful of God's goodness, and my sins are covered by the forgiving love of Christ crucified. I'm most thankful for the people I have met, and I only hope that they never have to grieve about me, but that they, too, will always be certain of, and thankful for God's mercy and forgiveness" (*Letters and Papers from Prison*, p. 393). Bonhoeffer would be hung in the Flossenbürg concentration camp on April 9, 1945, one month before the end of the war in Europe.

As I read this part of Bonhoeffer's letter, it struck me that it could be seen as a 20th century expression of what we read in I Peter this morning. The author of this letter is writing to Christians who are dispersed throughout the Roman Empire and who, because of their faith, are finding life difficult, if not altogether painful. Peter reminds his readers of the nature of their inheritance: "By his great mercy he has given us a new birth into a living hope through the resurrection of Jesus Christ from the dead, ... In this you rejoice, even if now for a little while you have had to suffer various trials, so that the genuineness of your faith...may be found to result in praise and glory and honor when Jesus Christ is revealed" (I Peter 1:3b, 6, 7).

What's powerful about this passage is that it does not deny the reality – the often painful reality – of life. And in the midst of that reality, the gospel is nonetheless true. It is what Flannery O'Connor called "Christian realism." A devout Catholic who took God and the gospel seriously, O'Connor wrote stories about people who were not nice folk. In some of her letters she expressed amusement when people would occasionally ask why she always wrote about bad people...why couldn't she write about nice people? they would ask. It was this tension, or struggle, between the Christian faith in a God of grace and mercy, on the one hand, and the real world that was often so very cruel that fascinated O'Connor.

In a letter of August 9, 1955 she wrote of the freedom the church should encourage for people to deal honestly with issues of the world that trouble people. She cited a priest who had said that someone should "not come into the Church until he [or she] felt it would be an enlargement of his [or her] freedom" (*The Habit of Being*, p. 93). Isn't it strange that, for many, the church represents a restriction or confinement or limitation rather than an enlargement of the freedom God offers us?

"By his great mercy he has given us a new birth into a living hope through the resurrection of Jesus Christ from the dead, and into an inheritance that is imperishable, undefiled, and unfading, ..." That inheritance is the legacy we have received. New birth. A living hope. Freedom to face, and live in, the world with all its threats and fears and uncertainties. As the Heidelberg Catechism puts it in response to the first question, "What is your only comfort, in life and in death?", "That I belong – body and soul, in life and in death – not to myself but to my faithful Savior, Jesus Christ, ..." That is what gives meaning to life. That is why we are free to embrace the church – not because it has all the answers, but because it is precisely there that we can search and wonder and be honest about whatever questions and doubts we might have.

Baron Friedrich von Hügel, who had an Austrian father and a Scottish mother and whose life bridged the 19th and 20th centuries, described God as "a stupendously rich Reality" (*The Life of Prayer*, p. 8). I think Dietrich Bonhoeffer and Flannery O'Connor would not only agree with that understanding of God, but might also say that the stupendously rich reality of God makes all the difference in how we see what most people would call "the real world."

This morning we also read Psalm 16. Central to that psalm are the words: "The Lord is my chosen portion and my cup; you hold my lot. The boundary lines have fallen for me in pleasant places; I have a goodly heritage" (Psalm 16:5-6). The "goodly heritage" that is ours is that we are part of the story that began with Adam and Eve and continues through John of Patmos and those suffering Christians he was addressing in the book of Revelation. The "goodly heritage" that is ours is the faith that has been passed on to us from parents, grandparents, and others who have influenced us. Of course, we do not accept it blindly. We have the responsibility to decide for ourselves what we believe, but that is part of the freedom that the church offers. The "goodly heritage" that is ours is the realization that the gospel that was heard and accepted for generations long before we came along is also intended for you and me and for all people. The "goodly heritage" that is ours is taking seriously the command Jesus gave his disciples in that upper room, that we love one another as he has loved us. (John 13:34), that we see in others the face of Christ, that we not judge or look with disdain on someone else, but treat them with the same grace with which we would hope to be treated.

Every Sunday we sing the doxology following the offering. It is a way of giving thanks to God for God's many gifts to us as well as giving thanks for the opportunity we have to give a portion of those gifts as well as ourselves to God's work. In reviewing the meaning of that original Greek word for doxology – doxa – we find these descriptions: glory, splendor, grandeur, power, kingdom, praise, honor; brightness, brilliance, revealed presence of God, among others. That's the kind of inheritance being described in the passage from I Peter. It's that description of the God to whom we belong that is our "goodly heritage." We get to be a part of this marvelous enterprise known as the Christian faith and the church.

"Although you have not seen him, you love him; and even though you do not see him now, you believe in him and rejoice with an indescribable and glorious joy, ..." In a few moments we will sing one of the great hymns of the church, a hymn that is usually reserved for All Saints Day. But it occurred to me that the words to this hymn, "For All the Saints", capture the sense of joyful struggle that the Christian life is and which is our inheritance. While we give thanks for the witness of those who have gone before us, we also acknowledge the fact that now it's our turn, we're "up", as it were, and while we are grateful for those who have gone before us, we have to make our own way. The hymn speaks of God's presence and guidance for our predecessors in the faith. In doing so, it expresses the trust that that same presence and guidance is there for us. Two of the stanzas are:

> "That wast their rock, their fortress, and their might;
> thou, Lord, their captain in the well-fought fight;
> thou, in the darkness drear, their one true light.
> Alleluia! Alleluia!

> "And when the strife is fierce, the warfare long,
> steals on the ear the distant triumph song,
> and hearts are brave again, and arms are strong.
> Alleluia! Alleluia!"

Each stanza ends with that word "Alleluia!" It is a way of saying that no matter how we may experience this life, the final word is always one of doxology and praise – Alleluia!

Our legacy is one of doxology – giving thanks for the stupendously rich reality of God and the joyful opportunity to be a part of the gospel of Jesus Christ and his love for the world. What a magnificent legacy that has been entrusted to us!

Thanks be to God!

Harvey

Habakkuk 3:17-19

September 3, 2017

Though the fig tree does not blossom, and no fruit is on the vines; though the produce of the olive fails, and the fields yield no food; though the flock is cut off from the fold, and there is no herd in the stalls, yet I will rejoice in the Lord; I will exult in the God of my salvation. God, the Lord, is my strength; he makes my feet like the feet of a deer, and makes me tread upon the heights.

"Harvey" was first a play, running on Broadway for three years from 1944-1947. In 1950 they made it into a movie. In both Jimmy Stewart played the lead as Elwood P. Dowd. You may recall that Elwood has an imaginary friend – a six foot, three inch rabbit – which, of course, only Elwood can see and talk to. The rabbit's name is Harvey. Because no one else can see this friend, Elwood's sister, Veta, thinks Elwood has lost his mind and tries to have him committed to a mental institution. There are several lines from the movie that are memorable, but I'd like to mention two of them. In an interview with the psychiatrist, Elwood says, "Well, I've wrestled with reality for 35 years, Doctor, and I'm happy to state I finally won out over it." The second, perhaps more well-known and theologically more important one, is this: "Years ago my mother used to say to me, she'd say, 'In this world, Elwood, you must be '– she always called me Elwood –' In this world, Elwood, you must be oh so smart or oh so pleasant. 'Well, for years I was smart. I recommend pleasant. You may quote me." Incidentally, by the end of the movie it's Elwood's sister – the "sane one," that ends up being institutionalized, not Elwood.

Over the past ten days the people of southeast Texas had a visit from another Harvey, and one not nearly as pleasant as Elwood P. Dowd or his friend, the imaginary rabbit. While some of us in this particular area suffered some damage if not loss of property, it must be said that most of us survived the fear of rising water, the terror of tornado warnings, and the uncertainty of life from one moment to the next. We must be careful about using that phrase, "we are blessed" because what does that say about those who have suffered and lost so much? Does it not make more sense simply to say that we are grateful? Suppose we had not been as fortunate as we are? Would we say that we were not blessed by God?

The first passage that was read this morning are final verses of chapter 12 of Paul's letter to the church at Corinth, immediately before the chapter on love. Paul uses the human body to describe the harmonious way in which the church is to work. Each part contributes to the health of the whole body. Hands have their function. Eyes have their function. Ears have their function. And when one part of the body suffers, all suffer together, and when one part of the body is honored, the whole body rejoices. I mention this because some of us were feeling guilty that we, as individuals and as a church, were not doing enough to alleviate the pain and hurt of others. We were trying to stay in touch with our own members to make sure everyone was okay and to determine what kind of damage had been done to their homes. Then we heard about a spontaneous response by the Connect Community Church across the street. After a post on Facebook, several people gathered up clothes and toiletries and delivered them to that church. Then some of us delivered these items to different reception centers. For whatever reason – whether guilt or a genuine desire to help others – the cities of Pasadena and throughout the greater Houston area responded with remarkable generosity. But, as someone else has said, now the hard work of recovery and rebuilding actually begins. With the number of volunteers overwhelming now, it may be that the time volunteers are needed will be in the next couple of weeks and months. Not every church needs to be a shelter. Not every church needs to be a distribution center. Not everyone can do all the jobs that will be needed to be done. But each of us can do something, even if it's checking in with people over the phone.

The Scripture reading from Habakkuk forms the closing verses to that prophetic book. Prophesying about 600 years before the birth of Jesus, Habakkuk questioned God's justice as he saw the Babylonians overrunning various little kingdoms, including the tiny kingdom of Judah. Why would God allow such things to happen? Why does God allow such things as floods and tornadoes to happen, not only in southeast Texas but in Mumbai, India as well? Why does God allow ruthless tyrants to torture their constituents? Why does God allow this and allow that? "Why do the wicked prosper?" is asked by the psalmist as well as the prophets. "How can we sing the Lord's song in a strange land?" the psalmist asks reflecting the pain of a people in exile. It is the perennial question generations ask. It's the question Job asked, one to which his companions could not offer a satisfactory answer. Interestingly, while many are quick to ask why things seem to go wrong, rarely do people ask why they may be the beneficiaries of good fortune. Or, if they do, it's either because they are such good people or because God has somehow favored them, neither answer of which is satisfactory from a biblical or theological point-of-view. The apostle Paul takes a different approach. He seems to take suffering as an honor, especially if it is caused by his proclamation of the gospel. No self-pity there.

And yet, while it remains a mystery for the prophet, note how Habakkuk concludes: "Though the fig tree does not blossom, and no fruit is on the vines; though the produce of the olive fails, and the fields yield no food; though the flock is cut off from the fold, and there is no herd in the stalls, yet I will rejoice in the

Lord; I will exult in the God of my salvation. God, the Lord, is my strength; he makes my feet like the feet of the deer, and makes me tread upon the heights" (Habakkuk 3:17-19). The prophet seems to be saying that God is God and God is good, no matter what happens to me or to us or to anyone.

If that's the case – and we affirm with Habakkuk that it is – then we are not to be paralyzed by questions that serve no useful purpose. Rather, we are to be up and about loving and serving our neighbors, whoever they may be. Some questions are good and useful ones, and some serve no useful purpose at all.

David Esterline is the president of Pittsburgh Theological Seminary. In a recent thought piece he wrote about the closing two verses in the book of Acts. The English reads: "He [Paul] lived there [Rome] two whole years at his own expense and welcomed all who came to him, proclaiming the kingdom of God and teaching about the Lord Jesus Christ with all boldness and without hindrance" (Acts 28:30-31). Esterline notes that the phrase "without hindrance" comes from one Greek word that can also be translated "without intimidation" ("President's Communique" in a Seminary email, dated 9-1-17). It seems to me that that is exactly what Habakkuk is calling his listeners to do. Regardless of the circumstances, we are to live and proclaim the kingdom or, as Esterline says, "without intimidation." Circumstances should not intimidate us or cause us to lose courage. The gospel is the gospel, whether things are a disaster for us or not. And if they are not a disaster for us, we are not called to relax, but rather we are called to pour even more energy into living and proclaiming God's love and kingdom.

Elwood P. Dowd's mother said, "In this world you must be oh so smart or oh so pleasant." Elwood's answer, I would argue, is a testament to the way God would want us to live. "Well, for years I was smart. I recommend pleasant. You may quote me." God calls us to be pleasant in all circumstances, whether the fig tree blossoms or not, whether there is fruit on the vine or not, whether our houses were flooded or not.

Thanks be to God!

Who Are Those Guys Anyway?

Luke 10:25-37

Just then a lawyer stood up to test Jesus. "Teacher," he said, "what must I do to inherit eternal life?" He said to him, "What is written in the law? What do you read there?" He answered, "You shall love the Lord your God with all your heart, and with all your soul, and with all your strength, and with all your mind; and your neighbor as yourself." And he said to him, "You have given the right answer; do this, and you will live."

But wanting to justify himself, he asked Jesus, "And who is my neighbor?" Jesus replied, "A man was going down from Jerusalem to Jericho, and fell into the hands of robbers, who stripped him, beat him, and went away, leaving him half dead. Now by chance a priest was going down that road; and when he saw him, he passed by on the other side. So likewise a Levite, when he came to the place and saw him, passed by on the other side. But a Samaritan while traveling came near him; and when he saw him, he was moved with pity. He went to him and bandaged his wounds, having poured oil and wine on them. Then he put him on his own animal, brought him to an inn, and took care of him. The next day he took out two denarii, gave them to the innkeeper, and said, 'Take care of him; and when I come back, I will repay you whatever more you spend.' Which of these three, do you think, was a neighbor to the man who fell into the hands of the robbers?" He said, "The one who showed him mercy." Jesus said to him, "Go and do likewise."

Some of you may remember the 1969 movie "Butch Cassidy and the Sundance Kid". It's the story, based loosely on fact, of two outlaws -- Robert LeRoy Parker and Harry Longabaugh -- and their escapades in the late 1890s in Wyoming and, eventually, in Bolivia where they continued their exploits by robbing banks. After two train robberies and an unsuccessful attempt to hide out, the two find themselves on the run, trying to escape the clutches of a posse led both by a lawman and an Indian tracker by the name of "Lord Baltimore". Eventually, Butch, played by Paul Newman, and Sundance, played by Robert Redford, find themselves at the edge of a very high cliff, below which are the rushing waters of a powerful river. When Sundance confesses that he cannot swim, Butch says not to worry because the fall itself would probably kill them.

As the two tried to escape the posse, they kept turning around, hoping that they would escape their pursuers. Much to their surprise, in the distance they realized that they had not gotten rid of them. Occasionally, upon seeing the posse in the distance, Butch would mutter, "Who are those guys anyway?" About that time they reached the cliff, survived the fall, and made their escape. Actually, some of the posse came from the Pinkerton Detective Agency, hired by banks and railroad companies in an attempt to recover the money Butch and Sundance had absconded with and to arrest them for their actions.

"Who are those guys anyway?" I wonder what might have gone through the mind of that innkeeper when the unnamed Samaritan brought the wounded man and left him to be cared for. While it is only a parable, Jesus' stories invite us into the stories he tells. Who was that Samaritan anyway? We don't even have a name to give him. Just a Samaritan. Let's call him Sam. Clearly, Sam was more than simply a Samaritan. In this day of identity politics in which people are identified simply by their ethnic identity or their country of origin or the language they speak or their political persuasion, Jesus tells us only that Sam was a Samaritan – one of those persons whom good Jews despise. And that's what makes the story effective, isn't it? The man is identified only as a Samaritan. Everyone knew that a wall of indifference, if not hatred, existed between Jews and Samaritans due mainly to the Israelites' belief that, though they had a common heritage, the Samaritans had bought in to other religious beliefs. The Samaritans were considered to be foreigners Nothing more need be known. Kind of like the way many today see persons from certain other countries.

I suspect that that innkeeper was suspicious of Sam as soon as he entered the door. Maybe his first thought was that Sam had beaten up this Jew. But if that were the case, why would Sam bother to bring him into town, pay for his care, and then promise to pay even more later if it was required? We don't know what that innkeeper thought, and for the purposes of Jesus 'story, I suppose it's not important. And yet, surely he and anyone else who might have seen Sam and his mule carrying the wounded man into town must have wondered, Who is this guy anyway?

Could it even be what it appears to be? The story is reminiscent of Nathanael's retort to Philip when Philip tells him that he has come across the one "about whom Moses in the law and also the prophets wrote, Jesus son of Joseph from Nazareth" (John 2:45). You remember Nathanael's response? "Can anything good come out of Nazareth?" The psalmist picks up this theme with the words, "The stone that the builders rejected has become the chief cornerstone" (Psalm 118:22). And Isaiah depicts the Messianic servant in a similar way: "Who has believed what we have heard? And to whom has the arm of the Lord been revealed? For he grew up before him like a young plant, and like a root out of dry ground; he had no form or majesty that we should look at him, nothing in his appearance that we should desire him. He was despised and rejected by others; a man of suffering and acquainted with infirmity; and as one from whom others hide their faces he was despised, and we held him of no account" (Isaiah 53:1-3).

The question we are posing to the Samaritan could just as well be posed to all the characters in this story, including the wounded man whom the Samaritan helps. Who are these guys anyway? There's a sense in which they all represent the church. We are all neighbors called to help and serve one another, and not only one another, but those whom we label, whom we stereotype, whom we judge. The wounded one may indeed be the Christ figure.

This church's Brunch and Book Group just discussed a novel by Fredrik Backman with the title *My Grandmother Asked Me to Tell You She's Sorry*. The central characters are Elsa, a 7-year-old girl, her grandmother who dies early in the story but who is very much part of the rest of the novel, and Elsa's mother. There are other characters that are important, but all somehow have a connection to Elsa's grandmother, and all seem to live in the same apartment complex. One of the characters is a woman in a black skirt who always appears to be drunk. We become weary of her constant screaming. Later in the book we learn that she is actually a psychotherapist and that her two sons and her husband had died in a tsunami. Well, that makes all the difference in how we viewed her. No longer simply an alcoholic, but now a grieving mother and wife. Judgmentalism has been transformed into sympathy and compassion.

We don't know what that Samaritan's story was. What we do know is that he is no longer simply "one of those Samaritans," but his actions revealed a side to him that forced others to reconsider, if not totally abandon, their previous superficial evaluation of him.

On this Dedication Sunday our pledge is a financial one, to be sure. However, our pledge is also to remember that, as followers of Jesus Christ, that one whom others rejected – and, truth be told, had we been there, we might well have rejected as well – we are to follow and serve. Jesus used the stereotypical Samaritan to show that stereotypes don't work. Everyone has a story. Everyone has baggage. But everyone is a child of God. And everyone is our neighbor. Therefore, we are called to treat everyone as if he or she were not only our neighbor, but Jesus Christ himself.

With all its faults and shortcomings, that's what the church is about – loving and serving God, loving and serving one another. That's what this church is about. We may have our stereotypical views of others, but they must be tempered by the gospel that they have a story and they are children of God, no less than we. May our financial pledge be only one part of our pledge to live with the kind of compassion, humility, grace, and love that Sam showed to the wounded and vulnerable man in that parable. That's what the church is called to be and do. May we live up to that Samaritan's example.

Thanks be to God!

What Language Shall I Borrow?

I John 1:1-2:2

April 8, 2018

We declare to you what was from the beginning, what we have heard, what we have seen with our eyes, what we have looked at and touched with our hands, concerning the word of life – this life was revealed, and we have seen it and testify to it, and declare to you the eternal life that was with the Father and was revealed to us – we declare to you what we have seen and heard so that you also may have fellowship with us; and truly our fellowship is with the Father and with his Son Jesus Christ. We are writing these things so that our joy may be complete.

This is the message we have heard from him and proclaim to you, that God is light and in him there is no darkness at all. If we say that we have fellowship with him while we are walking in darkness, we lie and do not do what is true; but if we walk in the light as he himself is in the light, we have fellowship with one another, and the blood of Jesus his Son cleanses us from all sin. If we say that we have no sin, we deceive ourselves, and the truth is not in us. If we confess our sins, he who is faithful and just will forgive us our sins and cleanse us from all unrighteousness. If we say that we have not sinned, we make him a liar, and his word is not in us.

My little children, I am writing these things to you so that you may not sin. But if anyone does sin, we have an advocate with the Father, Jesus Christ the righteous; and he is the atoning sacrifice for our sins, and not for ours only but also for the sins of the whole world.

I have had the opportunity to serve on two juries, one in Bell County and one in Fort Bend County. Both cases had to do with relatively minor offenses. In contrast to courtroom scenes we see on television or in movies, when we are simply observers in our den or living room, there is little distance, either physical or psychological, between participants in the courtroom. As a member of the jury, one must pay attention to what's being said – by the judge, by the attorneys, and by the witnesses. With all the evidence laid out and all the arguments made, we had to decide where the truth lay. Furthermore, we were told that we could draw no conclusion if the person on trial chose not to testify.

Those experiences came to mind as I read and reflected on the passage we read this morning from I John. It opens as if the writer were in the witness box: "We declare to you what was from the beginning, what we have heard, what we have seen with our eyes, what we have looked at and touched with our hands, concerning the word of life – this life was revealed, and we have seen it and testify to it, and declare to you the eternal life that was with the Father and revealed to us..." (I John 1:1-2). And, of course, the message that John proclaims is that God is light and calls us to live in the light, and that this God is a God of grace and forgiveness. If we were to continue to read this letter, we would discover a powerful testimony not only to the love God has for all of us, but that love is the very definition of God.

This is John's testimony to the early church, and it is an articulate one. He does it, he says, "so that our joy may be complete" (1:4). Interestingly, that is the same language Jesus uses in the Gospel of John (15:11) where, after describing his relationship with his disciples as one of his being the vine and they being the branches, he says, "I have said these things to you so that my joy may be in you, and that your joy may be complete."

In his book *Testimony* Tom Long writes that Christians are always on the witness stand – by what we say, by how we live, by how we treat others. He says, "We are not on the witness stand to grow the church, make ourselves look religious, or figure out legal strategy that will ensure that our side wins." "We are witnesses," Long writes, "and we are there for one and only one purpose: to tell the truth about what we have seen and heard." Furthermore, Long says, "Christians are on the witness stand to tell that story, not because it is a likely story or an advantageous piece of testimony, but because it is true" (p. 29). That is what John is up to, and that is what we are up to.

The story – the true story – can be told in lots of different ways. While the poet, Edgar Guest, has said, "I'd rather see a sermon than hear one any day," there are other ways the gospel story is told. Music is a powerful way of telling the story, whether it's a hymn or an anthem, whether it's "Morning Has Broken" or the "Hallelujah Chorus" or something like Jane Marshall's "My Eternal King", or the anthem the choir sang this morning, "Easter Angel Song" which is a most moving expression of the story that is straight from Scripture. Music touches our soul with the truth of the gospel, whether we are actually participating in the singing or simply listening.

And art can touch our soul as well. As Henri Nouwen discovered and has helped others to see, Rembrandt's "Return of the Prodigal" tells the story not only of Jesus' parable, but of God's forgiveness and love in a way that becomes more profound the closer one looks at that painting. The various depictions of the incarnation as well as the crucifixion are attempts to testify to the love of God for humanity. Matthias Grünewald's triptych of the crucifixion that has John the Baptist pointing to the crucified Jesus and saying, "He must increase while I must decrease" has had a profound effect on Christians as a way of bearing witness to the truth of the gospel.

Or consider the language of sculpture. Who cannot be moved by Michelangelo's "Pieta", a dead Jesus in the arms of his mother? Or, in a more modern vein, there is the depiction by Timothy Schmalz of Jesus as a homeless man asleep on a park bench.

In literature the story is told by such diverse writers as John Bunyan in his *Pilgrim's Progress*, Anne Lamott's autobiographical *Traveling Mercies*, Nadia Bolz Weber's *Accidental Saints*, the poetry of Francis Thompson and George Herbert, and various biographies of persons whose lives have exemplified faithfulness in their understanding of the gospel.

These are all attempts to testify to the truth of God's love and grace. And there are many, many more. The author of the medieval hymn "O Sacred Head, Now Wounded" describes both the futility and the variety of ways of bearing witness to God's love in the words of the last stanza: "What language shall I borrow to thank thee, dearest friend, for this thy dying sorrow, thy pity without end? O make me thine forever; and should I fainting be, Lord, let me never, never outlive my love to thee."

The hymn we will be singing in a few moments is by Ruth Duck, a modern hymn writer. The tune is a familiar one as the words capture the struggle between deep personal pain, on the one hand, and grace and forgiveness, on the other. As we see, it is filled with questions, but it also ends with a plea for God to forgive the offended one as well as the offender. It goes like this:

> God, how can we forgive when bonds of love are torn?
> How can we rise and start anew, our trust reborn?
> When human loving fails and every hope is gone,
> your love gives strength beyond our own to face the dawn.

When we have missed the mark, and tears of anguish flow,
how can you still release our guilt, the debt we owe?
The ocean depth of grace surpasses all our needs.
A priest who shares our human pain, Christ intercedes.

Who dares to throw the stone to damn another's sin,
when you, while knowing all our past, forgive again?
No more we play the judge, for by your grace we live.
As you, O God, forgive our sin, may we forgive.

"We declare to you what was from the beginning, what we have heard, what we have seen with our eyes, what we have looked at and touched with our hands, concerning the word of life – this life was revealed, and we have seen it and testify to it, and declare to you the eternal life that was with the Father and was revealed to us...." Regardless of how the story is told – in our words, in music, in art, in literature, in sculpture, or simply in how we live – it must be truly and honestly real and authentic. It must be our witness to the truth of the gospel. We are on the witness stand. It's a challenge, but it is also a joy, for in the end the gospel is truly good news.

Thanks be to God!

No More a Stranger of a Guest

John 10:11-18

April 22, 2018

Jesus said, "I am the good shepherd. The good shepherd lays down his life for the sheep. The hired hand, who is not the shepherd and does not own the sheep, sees the wolf coming and leaves the sheep and runs away – and the wolf snatches them and scatters them. The hired hand runs away because a hired hand does not care for the sheep. I am the good shepherd. I know my own and my own know me, just as the Father knows me and I know the Father. And I lay down my life for the sheep. I have other sheep that do not belong to this fold. I must bring them also, and they will listen to my voice. So there will be one flock, one shepherd. For this reason the Father loves me, because I lay down my life in order to take it up again. No one takes it from me, but I lay it down of my own accord. I have power to lay it down, and I have power to take it up again. I have received this command from my Father."

There are few images in Scripture more powerful or popular than that of the shepherd. The prophet Ezekiel paints the picture of God as the true shepherd and he warns against those in Israel who are "false shepherds" (ch. 34). And, of course, there is the psalm that many have heard so often that they can say it from memory – the 23rd Psalm. In the New Testament Jesus tells the parable of the lost sheep in the same series of parables that includes a lost coin and a wayward son (Luke 15).

Today's New Testament reading has Jesus identifying himself as "the good shepherd". There are other ways Jesus identifies himself in John's Gospel: the light of the world; the bread of life; the way, the truth, and the life; the gate; the resurrection and the life; the true vine. But it is as the shepherd – the good shepherd – that we often think of Jesus, which is quite interesting since, at least in our industrial, technologically-advanced society, there are not many sheep or shepherds, or at least they are not as central a part of the economy as they were in a more rural, agricultural economy. And yet, we take great comfort in that image.

Just this past Thursday morning I was on my way to Southeast Memorial Hospital to visit two parishioners. I was on the feeder street to Beltway 8 heading towards Old Galveston Road. As you know, there is a good deal of construction along there. I happened to be listening to a CD that had recordings by Marvin Gaspard, the former pianist and choir director at Westminster Presbyterian Church and current pianist and choir director at St. Luke's Presbyterian Church here in Houston. I was driving about 50 mph, and the car behind me was tailgating me in very heavy traffic. I gently tapped my brakes and the driver behind me made an obscene gesture to me. At that very moment the piece on the CD was "Savior, Like a Shepherd Lead Us". The contrast between driving in heavy Pasadena and Houston traffic and the pastoral image of sheep and shepherd in the midst of them could hardly have been starker. "Blessed Jesus, Blessed Jesus, much we need Thy tender care." Did I ever!

The interesting thing about this particular designation that Jesus attributes to himself is that it is the only one, as far as I can tell, that is relational. That is to say, to be a shepherd implies that there are sheep. The other "I am" statements are important about who Jesus is, but this one has to do with Jesus 'relationship with his sheep. Just as when someone says that he or she is a parent, we know that there are children, or when someone says that he or she is a grandparent or an aunt or an uncle, we know that there are relatives involved who are related to this person. So also, when Jesus says he is the good shepherd, we can assume that he relates to those whom he calls his sheep. Indeed, in our text immediately after calling himself the good shepherd, Jesus says, "The good shepherd lays down his life for the sheep." The good shepherd protects the sheep and tries to fend off any approaching menace to the flock.

In spite of the increased urbanization of this nation's and the world's population today, this image of shepherd and sheep to describe the relationship between Jesus and God's people is one that resonates with many of us, if only in our imagination. There are not many of us who have not felt lost or confused or powerless or vulnerable at one time or another – just like that sheep that wandered off in Luke's account (15:4-7). We like to think of ourselves as being in control of our lives. We like to think of ourselves like those whom Garrison Keillor describes in his Lake Wobegone stories where "the women are strong, the men are good-looking, and the children are above average." But deep inside we know the truth may lie elsewhere. And we take great comfort in that image of sheep belonging to a good shepherd.

The distance between us and the life of a homeless person is not very wide. Many of us have had an all too familiar experience with someone trapped in the vicious cycle of alcohol or drug addiction. Some of us may even have friends or relatives who have been there or who are in prison. And if we look closely enough, we can find within ourselves thoughts and words that make us not much different than those whom we judge or criticize. And yet, they are God's sheep as well. They have been made in the image of God, have they not? That distance becomes small indeed, if it does not vanish altogether.

Bob Lively, a good friend and now a retired Presbyterian minister who spent much of his ministry as a pastoral counselor, wrote a book about 20 years ago on how Psalm 23 can be seen as a kind of prescription God offers to relieve human stress and anxiety. Before he went into pastoral counseling, Bob was instrumental in beginning the Stewpot ministry at First Presbyterian Church in Dallas, a program that offered food to the homeless in downtown Dallas. It has expanded to provide shelter, medical care, and dental care to that same population. Those are the sheep, I think, that Jesus tended to and calls us to tend to. After all, did he not say, "Those who are well have no need of a physician, but those who are sick; I have come to call not the righteous but sinners" (Mark 2:17).

Do we not all fall into that category of sinners, perhaps especially those who think of themselves as being healthy – or righteous? So, the good shepherd lays down his life for his sheep and, as his sheep, we are called, first, to see all others as fellow-sheep, and, second, to care for each other, even – or especially – for those who are weary, lost, sick, or simply different from us.

Or consider the families of those who lost a son or a daughter in recent shootings in this country? Or those whose family members die serving their country overseas? Or those who simply find themselves living in a cycle of poverty and seem unable to escape it. Or those who are dealing with issues about which we may not know and, if we do know, cannot imagine their nightmare. There's no shortage of fear, anxiety, and brokenness around us.

If you haven't noticed already, all three hymns that we are singing today are based on the 23rd Psalm. As different as the tunes are, all three fit the words. They are ones that are pensive and offer comfort – just as the psalm itself does. I recall watching news coverage of the crash of the Pan American Flight 103 over Lockerbie, Scotland on December 21, 1988. A few days after that tragedy there was coverage of a worship service in a church in Lockerbie. The music and the voices that wafted over the wintry landscape of that small Scottish town were those of our opening hymn. You'll note that it comes from the Scottish Psalter of 1650. What comfort those words and that tune must have brought to families whose lives had been shattered by that horrific event.

It is, however, Isaac Watts 'adaptation of that psalm that I want to draw your attention, "My Shepherd Will Supply My Need". The last verse captures, I think, the sense of both the 23rd Psalm and Jesus 'words in John 10:

> The sure provisions of my God attend me all my days;
> O may your house be my abode, and all my work be praise.
> There would I find a settled rest, while others go and come;
> no more a stranger, or a guest, but like a child at home.

That last line reflects the gospel of the relationship between shepherd and sheep, between that one who brings health and wholeness and home to those whose lives have been broken, hopeless, and lost. "No more a stranger, or a guest, but like a child at home." That one who lays down his life for the sake of his sheep is the same one who, as Jesus says, takes it up again and offers new life. It's that relationship for which all of us yearn and, thankfully, it's in that relationship that we discover that we are no more a stranger, or a guest, but like a child at home.

Thanks be to God!

www.ingramcontent.com/pod-product-compliance
Lightning Source LLC
Chambersburg PA
CBHW071016120626
46546CB00003B/1119